KEY
WOMEN
WRITERS

H.D.

KEY
WOMEN
WRITERS
EDITOR: SUE ROE

H.D.
THE CAREER OF
THAT STRUGGLE

RACHEL BLAU DUPLESSIS

Associate Professor
Department of English
Temple University
Philadelphia

Indiana University Press
Bloomington and Indianapolis

Manufactured in Great Britain

Library of Congress Cataloging-in-Publication Data

DuPlessis, Rachel Blau.
  H.D., the career of that struggle.

  (Key women writers)
  Bibliography: p.
  1. H.D. (Hilda Doolittle), 1886–1961—Criticism
and interpretation. 2. Feminist literary criticism.
I. Title. II. Series.
PS3507.0726Z62 1986   811'.52   86-45393
ISBN 0-253-32702-4
ISBN 0-253-20400-3 (pbk.)

1 2 3 4 5 90 89 88 87 86

to Koré Simone DuPlessis

Titles in the Key Women Writers Series

Key Women Writers
Series Editor: Sue Roe

The *Key Women Writers* series has developed in a spirit of challenge, exploration and interrogation. Looking again at the work of women writers with established places in the mainstream of the literary tradition, the series asks, in what ways can such writers be regarded as feminist? Does their status as canonical writers ignore the notion that there are ways of writing and thinking which are specific to women? Or is it the case that such writers have integrated within their writing a feminist perspective which so subtly maintains its place that these are writers who have, hitherto, been largely misread?

In answering these questions, each volume in the series is attentive to aspects of composition such as style and voice, as well as to the ideas and issues to emerge out of women's writing practice. For while recent developments in literary and feminist theory have played a significant part in the creation of the series, feminist theory represents no specific methodology, but rather an opportunity to broaden our range of responses to the issues of history, pyschology and gender which have always engaged women writers. A new and creative dynamics between a woman critic and her female subject has been made possible by recent developments in feminist theory, and the series seeks to reflect the

vii

important critical insights which have emerged out of this new, essentially feminist, style of engagement.

It is not always the case that literary theory can be directly transposed from its sources in other disciplines to the practice of reading writing by women. The series investigates the possibility that a distinction may need to be made between feminist politics and the literary criticism of women's writing which has not, up to now, been sufficiently emphasized. Feminist reading, as well as feminist writing, still needs to be constantly interpreted and re-interpreted. The complexity and range of choices implicit in this procedure are represented throughout the series. As works of criticism, all the volumes in the series represent wide-ranging and creative styles of discourse, seeking at all times to express the particular resonances and perspectives of individual women writers.

Sue Roe

Contents

This is the central struggle of the woman writer. For every word, each cadence, each posture, the tone, the range of voices, the nature of plot, the rhythm of structures, the things that happen, events excluded, the reasons for writing, the way she's impeded, the noises around her, vocabularies of feeling, scripts of behaviour, choices of wisdom, voices inside her, body divided, image of wonder

all must be remade. [. . .]

It was the struggle not to be reduced, to be neither muse nor poetess.

It is the struggle. The career of the woman poet is the career of that struggle.

> ('Family, Sexes, Psyche: an essay on H.D. and
> the muse of the woman writer', *Montemora* 6
> (1979), pp. 141, 145)

Foreword

Condensed to the point of at least my intense frustration, ignoring certain texts by H.D. and by other writers which might further illuminate these issues, this book aims to be just about what it was asked to be: an overview of H.D.'s literary career informed by the new feminist criticism. It could not have been written without primary biographical, historical and critical work by an array of contemporary rediscoverers of H.D., tireless workers in archives and texts: Susan Stanford Friedman, L.S. Dembo, Robert Duncan, Albert Gelpi, Susan Gubar, Barbara Guest, Deborah Kelly Kloepfer, Adalaide Morris, Alicia Ostriker, Vincent Quinn, and others. The H.D. issue of *Contemporary Literature* (1969) under the editorship of L.S. Dembo is to be credited with impelling this generation of work. Perdita Schaffner, H.D.'s daughter, deserves generous and heart-felt thanks. Nor could this book exist without communities of feminists and their brave, emergent thought. My home institution, Temple University, contributed a Grant-in-Aid of Research (1983–85) which assisted me with this project. The hospitality of Beinecke Library, Yale University, which holds most of H.D.'s unpublished manuscripts and letters, is very gratefully acknowledged. And the book occurs in the hope that more complete histories of modernism than now exist will be (numerously) written with the

H.D.

intertextualities of gender explored and illuminated, with women writers properly in place and even, at times, foregrounded.

Preface

Four kinds of authority are at issue for women writers: cultural authority, authority of otherness/marginality, gender authority, and sexual/erotic authority. Each of these issues is particularly inflected with a woman's race, class and social condition. These questions of authority occur in no developmental order; they recur in variant and evolving ways; they are, assuredly, intertwined. Yet the interpretive and formal fiction upon which this book depends will make a specific question of authority correspond to each of four identifiable phases of H.D.'s poetic career. To define these phases, I have proposed some simple issues about the author, the kinds which, however, someone might want investigated: what did 'Greece' or antiquity mean to her? Why was she not always–or indeed very long–an 'imagist'? Why did she write all those novels, that prose? What was the meaning of her analysis with Freud? What functions did her re-animation of myth serve? What is the wary spirit of Eros which broods and flashes in her *oeuvre*? What is the trajectory of her career as a whole?

This study draws on feminist literary criticism and the analysis of culture. In its attempt to situate the life's work, or *oeuvre*, of a writer in the context of a life-work, or self-conscious personal struggles, I draw by way of inspiration on feminist 'new biography'.[1] Putting women

at the centre of inquiry, and examining with empathetic *Verstehen* as well as a critical scrutiny the strategies of a
life and the intersections of texts with lives, such a
criticism would ask: What are the material and
emotional conditions by which H.D. as a woman writer
did her work? How, to cite Rich, were 'the energies of
creation and relation' situated in her?[2] What conflicts
faced her? What was the shape of crises about love,
identity, vocation? What was her early mentoring, and
with what agendas? What were her sexualities and their
dilemmas, marriage, motherhood, and other choices of
role with their effects on the poetic career? How does
gender interact with political issues, her ties to artistic or
social movements, her setting of personal priorities and
tasks, her resistances to and confrontations with her
own powers? What were her imaginative and cultural
constructs about literature and about the writer?

The formation of a woman writer and her literary
career are subjects receiving intensified attention because of feminist critical work. Myra Jehlen has made
the persuasive suggestion that how a woman writer
creates and re-creates the possibility of her creativity is a
central site for investigation. These 'repeated acts' are
not only 'anterior to' the actual literary production, the
evidence of their existence is sealed in the literary career.
Jehlen further insists that these acts are not a purely
psychological manoeuvre which might be relegated only
to biography; they are 'conceptual' and 'linguistic': a
matter of situating the self in relation to conventions of
representation and then of constructing various 'enabling relationships' with, and in, language.[3] For H.D. –
and other women writers – these creative acts I have
summarised as four struggles for authority.[4]

Two related areas of inquiry will also take the whole
book to elucidate: How are these biographical and

material conflicts, issues and resolutions inscribed or encoded in individual texts: in image, plot, character, narrative movement, resolution, and in choice of modes (poetry, novel, memoir)? And: What are her attitudes to dominant discourses of women, sexuality and gender?

Acknowledgements

The author gratefully acknowledges permission to reprint passages from the following works:

Collected Poems: 1912–1944 by H.D. Copyright © 1982 by the estate of Hilda Doolittle. Reprinted by permission of New Directions Publishing Corporation and Carcanet Press, Manchester, England.

Bid Me to Live by H.D. © 1960 by N.H. Pearson. © 1983 The Estate of Hilda Doolittle. Copyright © 1983 by Perdita Schaffner; Copyright © 1983, Black Swan Books Ltd, Redding Ridge, CT. Published by Virago Press Ltd 1984. Reprinted by permission of Black Swan Books Ltd. and of Virago Books.

End to Torment by H.D. Copyright © 1979 by New Directions Publishing Corporation. Reprinted by permission of New Directions Publishing Corporation and Carcanet Press.

The Gift by H.D. Copyright © 1969, 1982 by the Estate of Hilda Doolittle. Copyright © 1982 by Perdita Schaffner. Published by Virago Press Ltd 1984. Reprinted by permission of New Directions Publishing Corporation and of Virago Books.

Hedylus by H.D. Copyright © 1928, 1980 by the Estate of Hilda Doolittle; Copyright © 1980 by New Directions Publishing Corporation; Copyright © 1980 by Perdita

Schaffner; Copyright © 1980 by Black Swan Books
Ltd. Reprinted by permission of Black Swan Books
Ltd.

Helen in Egypt by H.D. Copyright © 1961 by Norman
Holmes Pearson. Reprinted by permission of New
Directions Publishing Corporation and Carcanet
Press.

Hermetic Definition by H.D. Copyright © 1972 by Norman
Holmes Pearson. Reprinted by permission of New
Directions Publishing Corporation and Carcanet
Press.

HERmione by H.D. Copyright © 1982 by the Estate of
Hilda Doolittle. Copyright © 1981 by Perdita
Schaffner. Published (as HER) by Virago Press Ltd
1984. Reprinted by permission of New Directions
Publishing Corporation and of Virago Books.

Letters and Manuscripts of H.D. Printed by permission
of Perdita Schaffner and the Collection of American
Literature, The Beinecke Rare Book and Manuscript
Library, Yale University.

Letter of H.D. to William Carlos Williams, 1907.
Printed by permission of Perdita Schaffner. Cited
with the permission of The Poetry/Rare Books
Collection of the University Libraries, State University of New York at Buffalo.

Letter of H.D. to May Sarton, 17 August 1939.
Printed by permission of Perdita Schaffner. Cited
with the permission of the Henry W. and Albert A.
Berg Collection; The New York Public Library; Astor,
Lenox and Tilden Foundations.

Letter of H.D. to Marianne Moore, 27 June [1940].
Printed by permission of Perdita Schaffner. Cited by
permission of The Rosenbach Museum and Library.

Notes on Thought and Vision and The Wise Sappho by H.D.
Copyright © 1982 by the Estate of Hilda Doolittle,

Brief Chronology of H.D.'s Life

1886   Born, 10 September, Bethlehem, Pennsylvania

1895   Moves just outside of Philadelphia; H.D.'s father, Professor Doolittle, heads Flower [Astronomy] Observatory

1903   Graduates from Friends Central High School

1905   Attends Bryn Mawr College for three terms

1907   Having met Erza Pound about five years before this, she is now engaged to him. Also knows William Carlos Williams

1911   With the engagement to Pound broken, strong ties to Frances Gregg, she embarks for Europe with Gregg and her mother.

1912   First poems admired by Pound

1913   First publication as H.D., Imagiste. Marries Richard Aldington

1915   Stillbirth of Aldington's child

1916   Publishes first book, *Sea Garden*. Strong ties to D.H. Lawrence. Aldington serving in army. H.D. takes over as assistant editor of *The Egoist*

1918   Lives with Cecil Gray; pregnant with his child. First meeting with Bryher. Brother killed in war. Marriage ends in separation

1919   Frances Perdita Aldington born, after mother survives influenza. Brief reconciliation of the Aldingtons, but Richard seem both war-shocked and increasingly enraged about the child. After hallucinatory experiences, writes *Notes on Thought and Vision*

1920   Relationship with Bryher in earnest; they are bonded the rest of H.D.'s life, ceasing to live together after 1946

1920–23   Much travelling with Bryher: Corfu, United States (including California), Greece, Egypt. Bryher marries Robert McAlmon in 1921. H.D. works on first novels

1927   H.D.'s mother, Helen, dies. POOL films and *Close Up* begin. Bryher (divorced from McAlmon) marries Kenneth Macpearson. *HERmione* written

1930   Acts in *Borderline* with Paul Robeson

1931   Begins psychotheraphy in London

1933   Enters analysis with Sigmund Freud; another set of sessions in 1934. Publishes novellas from 'Borderline' group

1938   Divorced from Richard Aldington.

1939   Writes *Bid Me to Live*

1940   Spends the war years in London, including under Blitz, writing *The Gift* (1941–43) and *Trilogy* (1942–44)

1945   Connection to Hugh Dowding; spiritualist seances; first publication of part of *Tribute to Freud*

1946   Severe breakdown; enters Küsnacht Klinik, Switzerland

1949   Major self-assessment of recent work

1952–54   Writes *Helen in Egypt*; tie to Erich Heydt

1955   Writes *Compassionate Friendship*

1956   Seventieth birthday in United States; first trip there in 35 years

1958–59   *End to Torment* and 'Winter Love' written

1960   'Hermetic Definition' written; in USA to receive American Academy of Arts and Letters medal (first woman to receive it)
1961   Dies in Switzerland; buried in Nisky Hill Cemetery, Bethlehem, Pennsylvania

Chapter One

'Sheer young classicism
circa 1917'

> Rome and the outposts of Rome. That runs in my head,
> arma virumque, that beats down the battered fortress of
> my brain, cano. I sing of arms and a God. . . . What do I sing?
> I don't know what I sing. What anyhow does it matter what
> I sing, I, a nebulous personality without a name.
>
> (*Paint it To-day* (1920) III, 7)[1]

When one treats women writers as a group, or as
women, there are numerous questions as to where
'differences' lie, especially when some women writers
themselves (though not H.D.) resist any gesture to
gender, claim indifference to difference. Upon examination, difference may seem notably overdetermined:
socially, in special elements of female history and
women's social position, in female subculture and a
complex of (even contradictory) values formed in
response to reigning gender norms.[2] In the epigraph
above are arms and a man, even arms and a God; the
woman whose head is battered by these imperious,

1

imperial reminders tries a voice already enunciating heard epic melodies.

Difference may lie in gender formation through education and in the family. H.D. (1886–1961) mulled her family with special intensity and brilliance in essay-memoirs which trace patterns of love and power, election and failure inextricably mixed with gender: with being the only girl among brothers and half-brothers, with having powerful, gender-polarised parents, and as inextricably mingled with religion, myth, fairy-tales and other notable stories of spiritual resonance.

> . . . this triangle, this family romance, this trinity which follows the recognized religious pattern: *Father*, aloof, distant, the provider, the protector – but a little un-get-at-able, a little too far away and giant-like in proportion, a little chilly withal; *Mother*, a virgin, the virgin, that is, an untouched child, adoring, with faith, building a dream, and the dream is symbolized by the third member of the trinity, the *Child*, the doll in her arms.[3]

Difference exists in sets of female psychological and spiritual responses (as above, the covert claim to be the blessed Child, that is, Christ) which explore the ascribed status of other – that baseline of Western civilisation – or probe interlocks of marginalities, among which gender is notable, but which, for H.D., included bisexuality, expatriation, a particularist religious heritage (the Moravian), and enough wealth to live without paid employment. And, of course, the choice to become a writer.

Gilbert and Gubar suggest that the 'anxieties of authorship' besetting women because of their ideological and psychological heritage may issue in a shared project. Women writers may undertake to reshape the literary tradition by the hard labour of 'translation, transcription, and stitchery, re-vision and recreation'.[4] This metonymic analysis which postulates a unity of the domestic tasks of immanence with the spiritual and literary tasks of transcendence offers a formulation peculiarly appropriate to H.D. who translated and transposed from the Greek, who read 'writing' everywhere, and whose own metaphor for her compulsive, determined work was stitchery. ' "Like working on a sampler", she confided, years later. "So many stitches and just so many rows, day after day. If I miss even one day, I drop a stitch and lose the pattern and I feel I'm never going to find it again".'[5]

A further line of feminist argument says that women writers develop in their difference an oblique relation to convention and language, not that there is any 'specific female literary practice' (although there have been many pressures to muting, to language choice, to the ladylike), but there is, aslant to reigning conventions, some 'emphasis added', some exaggeration of narrative or linguistic strategies, some turning to whatever strategies culture at large deems oppositional, some places in writing by or about women where 'the accent never falls where it does with a man'.[6]

In the citation heading this chapter from an unpublished short novel by H.D., the decentred self, the insistence on cultural anonymity and a rejection of the authority of both classics and war (in the Virgilian catchphrase extended, cunningly mistranslated) are features which define one of H.D.'s many eponymous artisthero/ines. Her song is strangely asserted by her denial that it matters, H.D.'s characteristic immodest effacement showing her characteristic arrogant humility. From the classics and their male stories, from the veiled or unfocused self to the shrug away of enterprise, nay, even identity, this citation suggests primary questions of voice, text and tradition for H.D.

'That Hellenic, avid, by way of the States, naked kind of thinking' is the subject of this chapter: some thematic meanings, functions and situational uses H.D. made of antiquity, first Greek, but also Roman and, importantly, Egyptian materials (P, p. 173).[7] This use was so marked that it remains the essential H.D. for numerous commentators, And for good reason.

She herself chose a poem with the lines 'Greek flower, Greek ecstasy' for her gravestone; the work she completed before her death, the magisterial long poem, *Helen in Egypt*, is relentlessly classicising in every nervy impulse and grain. H.D.'s works take daunting turns among *Ion*, *Hippolytus*, *Hedylus*, *Iphegenia*, 'Demeter', 'Cassandra', 'Circe', 'Leda', 'Eurydice', Sappho, Nossis, Theocritus, Euripides, and other real and imagined Greeks of varying states and conditions. As well as assuming such figures as personae, H.D. translated from the Greek–was praised for her work by T.S. Eliot.[8] She wrote, from 1918 (or even earlier) to 1920, a casual but vital set of (mainly unpublished) notes on various Greek authors.[9] H.D. extended this knowledge emotionally and analytically when, in 1927, for the first film journal, *Close Up*, she formulated a series of studies about the spiritual and political potential of cinema called 'The Cinema and the Classics'. In short, H.D. inspired herself repeatedly by engagement with Greek materials, imitated and reproduced them to produce herself as a writer. And, as this early classicising period waned in the later 1920s, she recapitulated the interwoven meanings of modernity and antiquity in two novels: *Palimpsest* (1926) and *Hedylus* (1926/1928 pub).

Being a woman writer in Western culture is, like 'the moon in your hands' a two-sided possession in which the responsibility to the invisible 'other-side of everything' was a gift–and challenge–which H.D. used her whole career to scry and decipher.[10] The criticism of women's work in poetry began with a necessary hypothesis of internal doubt and conflict, external pressure and denial most sharply summarised in Suzanne Juhasz's early formulation: 'the double bind of the woman poet': to be an effective woman and an effective poet are mutually contradictory.[11] This necessary baseline of analysis needs some modification by a postulate such as that contained in Alicia Ostriker's *Writing Like a Woman*: that although 'diminishment', 'fear' and 'self-division' can be visible in the work, and/or in internal resistances, women writers who take these issues as their subject and ground, make a transition between 'literary fear and literary courage'.[12]

To all agendas given by others, H.D. is characteristically both complicit and resistant. Being a poet in the first place was an answer to a question of prior possession by her father, and his high expectations for her career, like his, in science, hers as the next Marie Curie.[13] In adolescence her resistance rode on a two-gendered front: she abhorred the domestic science classes that all the girls except herself 'are going in for', as she said in a letter of 1907 to William Carlos Williams, yet flirtatiously wonders whether, on his visits, he will 'spend all [his] time playing with the cooks'.[14] Williams, remembering her at that era, gives an interesting clue to her apparent resistance ('provocative indifference') to femininity, among other norms: 'She dressed indifferently, almost sloppily and looked to a young man, not inviting – she had nothing of that – but irritating, with a smile'.[15]

Her general sense of failure pointed by her quick exit from Bryn Mawr College, which she briefly attended in

1905 in the same graduating class (1909) as Marianne Moore (with whom she had life-long, though not close ties) might have signalled her incapacity to be a 'New Woman'–careerist, even promiscuous – as well as an 'old', docile and daughterly. 'Shocked . . . to be flunked quite frankly in English', H.D. notes this as 'one of the spurs toward a determination to self-expression'.[16] Her passion for Frances Gregg in these early years was another claim to self-definition, and an overwhelming experience to which H.D. remained, in her own way, loyal, even stating that Bryher, her life-long companion, was a double of this original lesbian love. Gregg received H.D.'s first pastoral love poems. Ezra Pound, inspiring the European trip of 1911 taken with Gregg and naming her 'Imagiste' in 1913, liberated her from provincial Philadelphia (his native milieu also) and became the 'stimulus or scorpionic sting or urge' for H.D.'s focused ambition.[17]

H.D. began her official career as a writer with a crisis of naming and appropriation which resulted in odd resolutions: her own poetic mask and a complicated double function for her literary career. Chaste initials were for ever to conceal both a female (Hilda) and a comic name (Doolittle), of course, her father's name, famous in other fields. If these initials are her own invention, used in an early (1908) letter to William Carlos Williams, it also remains true that their use was solemnised by Pound, as both priest and 'bridegroom' in poetry of the newly dedicated 'Imagiste'.[18] As the story goes, H.D. had written a poem which Pound slashes, cuts, shortens, and finally authorises ('And he scrawled "H.D., Imagiste" at the bottom of the page').[19] 'H.D.' did eventually become the name which encompassed her whole *oeuvre*. But she had as secret statements, sometimes used in published works, various

6

pseudonyms – for example, A.D. Hill, Delia Alton, Rhoda Peter, John Helforth.[20] Over her whole career, she conceived of some of her work as not-H.D. and most of her work as not-imagist.

This Pound–H.D. conjuncture, with its six-year pre-history of love, is an initiatory moment for modernism and for its agendas of gender. It may have been a triumphal moment to have her status as a poet valued by the man who had before been most decidedly fascinated by her as woman and muse. But while Pound marked her transition from muse ('But Dryad . . . ') to maker ('this is poetry!'), his gesture also appropriates her work (ETT, 18). For once he helped to create her identity in vocation, this paradigmatic encounter in the British Museum tearoom re-created 'a literary tradition that depends on and reinforces the masculine orientation of language and of the poet'.[21] The confluence of modernist literary history with the self-presentation of male poets certainly compromises one's ability to discern the inter-textualities of modernism, even the possible primogeni-ture of the female, not the male, writer. Modernist diction may, in ways still to be fully elucidated, be indebted to female gender stances (in Stein, in Loy, in Moore). Marianne DeKoven, assimilating Kristeva, sees modernist 'experimental writing as anti-patriarchal' a stance necessary to rupture dominant culture by a focus on the signifier, not the signified, and interestingly initiated by a woman, Gertrude Stein.[22] Jeanne Kammer suggests that the modernist style in Dickinson, Moore and H.D. was born from the pressures of silence – 'habits of privacy, camouflage, and indirection' – which resulted in 'linguistic compression' and juxtaposition.[23]

If H.D. is both muse and co-worker, if she writes the poems Pound could not, yet assumes the name Pound confers, some interweaving of sexual and textual identities has occurred. The initiatory imagist poem offers two clues to the gender issues in H.D.'s early lyrics. First, its source was the Greek woman poet, Anyte of Tegea, whose epitaphs include one about crossroads, orchard, coast and spring – precisely the motifs H.D. transposed. Second, her husband Richard Aldington had also translated and reworked that poem, giving his translation the same title. Pound's role compounds the mix of sexual politics and textual poetics.[24] So 'Hermes of the Ways' points towards H.D.'s connection as a woman poet to a long-ago woman poet, and toward ties of sexuality and vocation with two contemporary male poets.

Given that the creation of H.D. and the creation of imagism mythically occurred at the very same moment, she was not just a poet among others, she was poet and perfect exemplar. Possession and the mixture of the sexual and textual were issues also in the tragi-comic *mésalliance* with Aldington (itself in part incited by Pound). Pregnant for the second time (the first child, Aldington's died), H.D. is shut out of Aldington's bohemian 'open marriage'. She becomes (for him) Cecil Gray's 'girl'. As Pound had earlier, Aldington also attempts to seal her as his ideal, as he criticises both her recent writing ('less maturity than your early work') and her spelling errors. 'Remember [he writes from the front] H.D. cannot afford to be anything less than perfection'.[25] The former demand for her perfection returns her covertly to the status of muse, embodiment of an ideal to which others aspire, a role sacred to poetry as a social institution. Being either exemplar or muse presents startling problems; both together meant that a *mélange* of issues involving 'creation and relation' enter her early work (Rich, 'When We Dead Awaken', p.43).

The incident with Pound and Aldington's double-edged praise together show that H.D. had already (before the letter or the law of movement or manifesto) written poems that were definitionally 'imagist': spare, sinewy, direct; when Pound's were talky, explanatory, cluttered. Her work incited Pound both to the creation of poems and to the articulation of a poetics: direct, unabstract presentation of an emotion, non-ornamental structural use of images, a relative shrinking of poetic diction, with line-breaks and music following meaning.[26] Or, a list with imagist élan: 'precision, economy, concreteness, and stylistic innovation' (Quinn, 1967, p.23). Certain of Pounds's imagist poems – notably 'DORIA' and 'The Return' – seem Greek takes 'after' H.D., in all senses of that word. And Pound's early thoughts-on-his-feet about 'imagism' characterised the group as 'ardent Hellenists . . . pursuing interesting experiments in *vers libre*', a classicising definition most pertinent to H.D.[27]

Pound acknowledged his debt to H.D. in the 1914 extension of his poetic programme (the Vorticist Manifesto), importantly noting that the image 'causes form to come into being', an early assertion that imagism could become structural, leading to a long poem without rhetoric or filler, and with a relative suppression of syntactic or syntagmatic transitions, that is, prefiguring *The Cantos* poetics.[28] He cites H.D.'s 'Oread' in the Vorticist Manifesto, ranking it with Kandinsky and Picasso. That this seems a distinct overvaluation of that six-line poem should not blind us to an understanding of Pound's homage to the notable influence of H.D. Interestingly, compared with work contemporaneous with 'Oread', that poem is notably restrained in emotion and drama; other works in *The God* are closer to the tight expressionist despair of 'I am poisoned with rage of song' (CP, p.56). Susan Friedman has an elegant reading of the

9

poem, using it to illustrate both imagist principles and to prefigure psychoanalytic tenets: concision, condensation, displacement, fusion of contraries (Friedman, *Psyche Reborn*, pp.56–9).

H.D.'s role is muted or honorific in part because she wrote no statement on imagist poetics, no terse 'don'ts'; the 'didactic, polemical, and prescriptive' element in her (in contrast, say, to Mina Loy) is notably restrained, except, as Adalaide Morris has pointed out, in her sometimes hortatory analyses of cinema in the late 1920s.[29] H.D. avoids virtually any sense of polemic by a brilliant development of the essay form and its dialogic poetics. She may too have resisted manifesto by ambivalence to the imagist credo. In fact, her later statements – semi-historical in *Hedylus* and *Bid Me to Live*, autobiographical in *End to Torment* and semi-critical in *Notes on Thought and Vision* – take imagism apart, retaining its status as avatar of vision, but criticising the poetic rules and limits, hinting that the 'new' was really Greek, and quite old.[30] She called attention constantly to the gender politics of that poetic group in *Bid Me to Live*, especially the paralysing interplay between Aldington and D.H. Lawrence, with whom she was intensely but apparently platonically involved from 1914 to 1918. And she noted, in a 1916 review of a nominal imagist, her own heretical straining towards 'other and vaguer images . . . not that of direct presentation but that of suggestion' (Review of Fletcher, cited in Morris, 1984, p.417).

Indeed, *HERmione*, one of the works that summarises her poetic formation, encodes and criticises numerous imagist and pre-imagist poems by Pound, written at the time in loving adoration of herself, and uncannily preserved as *Hilda's Book*. By paraphrasing his poems in her prose, by encircling them, by analysing their sentiments of passion and possession, she makes her critique of his kind of love coextensive with a critique of his kinds of poetry.[31] Both are necessary to her formation as a writer. But this occurs by 1927; ten years earlier, her first negotiations attempted to see how far a beautiful and desirable young woman could go in combining making art and being artefact.[32] H.D. hints, in 1937, that the early poems are 'impelled by some inner conflict' (this would not be news about the works of any writer), but unfortunately she does not complete the analysis by identifying the conflict.[33] Here are some possibilities: love, desire and resistance; woman as poet or speaking subject and woman as desired object; control by others (whether family or lovers) and integrity of the self.

While certain time-honoured poetic stances are visible in H.D.'s early poetry, yearning for the ideal, pursuit and desire, pastoral engagements and a reading of natural landscapes, these are played out in new arenas formed by her gender. In a striking reading of Renaissance poetry which has implications for all works that allude richly to poetic tradition, Nancy Vickers implies that poetry itself as a literary mode presents certain gender narratives, and that tropes of beauty, love, nature, muse and time all reserve a particular place for gender. Discourses of woman are visually and mythically constructed by these overlapping strategies of representation; myths of desire and erotics, the poetic interest in depicting beauty, the idea that speaking is a form of erotic possession, and seeing in a scopic economy is set in relation to transgressing, propose women as 'bearers of meaning' than 'makers of meaning'.[34] This proposition makes an important problem and challenge for the woman poet.

Since, in H.D.'s case, one ineluctable force seems to

11

have been sexual desire, where to put the erotic, as a woman, and how to evoke cultural authority as a woman become linked problems, solved by an ecstatic 'encoding of active desire' which marks her poetry (Ostriker, 1983, p.13). On the one hand, her economy, not specular, is rather assimilative: translating is a way of infusing or transfusing one work into another; in another sense, using other poets' desires to state one's own means that desire is masked yet alleged. In addition, to affirm her authority, a woman writer could become both the Other as lover and the Other as writer–both Heliodora and Nossis.

'The minimal unit of poetic language is at least *double*, not in the sense of the signifier/signified dyad, but rather, in terms of *one and another*:[35] This, from Julia Kristeva, confronts us with the I/you relationship, resonant for H.D.'s work throughout, but peculiarly isolated in her intense, ritualistic early poems. Where to 'put' erotic energy, how to negotiate 'one and another' changes during the early works. *Sea Garden* (1916) as a title is already oxymoronic for vast/containment or uncontained cultivation, one suggestive of the 'scrutiny of dualisms' which Homans postulates as necessary to establish the female poetic voice. In the flower poems repeated through the manuscript, H.D. implies an argument with conventions of depiction. These flowers of the sea gardens are of a harsh surprising beauty, slashed, torn, dashed yet still triumphant and powerful, despite being wounded, hardened, tested by exposure. These flowers propose an almost contemptuous defiance of ease, of simple fashions of ripening. H.D. constructs flowers admired in ways and for motives far different from the view of lush ripeness in *carpe diem* roses.

In *Sea Garden*, however, an erotic plot is essayed, in which 'I' occurs in awed breathless yearning for an elusive 'you'. The 'you' might be a god or a person, spiritual traces or erotic pressures: significantly H.D. catches these forces just at the cusp of their disappearance, when they leave a sense of their energy and her yearning, their immanence and her half-answered desire, their power and her tribute, their spirit and her supplicating yet powerful ardour. She pushes herself to be the equal of the experience, even when it is marked with loss (Morris, 1984, pp.413–16). Yearning for the ideal (as in 'Cliff Temple' or 'Pursuit') plays with one masterplot of Graeco-Roman legend: pursuit, erotic conjuncture (or evasion) and metamorphosis. The sequence is collapsed into one endless pursuit with female power as stalker, reading the signs of the evasive but somewhat cruel other. 'But here/a wild-hyacinth stalk is snapped:/the purple buds – half ripe – /show deep purple/where your heel pressed' (CP, p.11). Whatever else might be said, this tactic prevents speaking or narrating being a form of possession of the 'you': it is precisely the opposite.

Especially in the interplay of the three goddesses, Aphrodite, Artemis and Athene, but in Apollo (Helios) as well, H.D. found acceptable names and characters for highly activated feelings of militant power, sexual resistance, personal austerity, sexual desire, arousal to bliss, and a debate between passion and autonomy which could be phrased, in 'classical' terms, as a struggle between Artemis and Aphrodite.

This lyric debate climaxes in *Hippolytus Temporizes* (1927), a long narrative poem or play, in which those two forces struggle and have, as in the myth, various chiastic and ironic successes. The work centres on a struggle between the two goddesses who are closer than either they or their main worshippers will admit until the crisis: Aphrodite (who has, of course, consumed

Phaedra) and Artemis (who spurns even the chaste and misanthropic love Hippolytus offers). But there is further complication. Both Artemis and Hippolytus have loved Hippolyta. Thus Artemis hates the son, who has linked Hippolyta to heterosexuality, while Hippolytus thinks his resemblance to his mother would be greatly tempting to Artemis. In the duplicitous exchanges characteristic of this plot, Aphrodite's woman, Phaedra, masquerades as Artemis, yet is not only successful at seduction, but is transfigured as that phosphorescent goddess. Artemis's man, Hippolytus, convinced that he has become a new Endymion, has none the less been deeply stung by erotic feeling. But, as the paired son–mother names reveal, heterosexuality is a skimpy cover for an incestuous longing by the son for the mother. So the sexualities immediate to H.D. involve some concerted probings into family romance which continued as her career unfolds.

Her nature poems are Greek dramas without any names of the goddesses, presenting a depersonalised abstract of antagonistic forces–as in 'Heat' (oft-anthologised), in which heat blunts fruits, fruits bear down, wind ploughs heat. Imbalances, struggles, pressures, resistances, not at all a mild version of cause and effect show in the interplay between desire, necessity and resistance. So, despite the unstinting Greek contexts and references, it is possible to see (as Norman Holmes Pearson has suggested) the whole set of lyrics only coincidentally Greek: the landscapes are American, the emotions are personal, the 'Greek' then becomes a conventional but protected projection of private feelings into public meanings.[36] H.D. offers this suggestion in the 1937 note on her early poetry: 'It is nostalgia for a lost land. I call it Hellas. I might, psychologically just as well, have listed the Casco Bay islands off the coast of

Maine . . . ' (*Oxford Anthology*, 1938, p.1287). But to 'call it Hellas' means 'it' (this special source for writing) is going by a version of her mother's name.

In the poems of 1917, set as a separate section in the *Collected Poems* of 1925, and then in *Hymen* (1921), the 'I' can be the voice of a strong female figure. The most powerful of these are antagonistic to the implied 'you' as they embark not on the pursuit of a sexual–spiritual epiphany (the literal presence of godhead) but on a hermeneutic quest: to reread themselves – 'Demeter', 'Eurydice', 'Simaethea' among these. And once they read, they reinterpret, become argumentative, want to present and prove correctives to former representations in art, ritual, myth. Demeter proves in her narrative that mother-love and its passionate kiss are more fundamental than sexual love and its rapacious desires. Eurydice proves that her apparent loss of life, earth and Orpheus are 'not loss', that she has more of her own 'light' without him than with. Here the 'one' distinguishes herself from 'another' – especially when that other has both erotic and cultural powers to define stories of desire and desires for story. Susan Friedman's powerful analysis of H.D.'s 'Helen' (1923) shows how although the main character is silent, the poet's voice and eye are committed to show the 'processes of masculine myth-making' that have swirled and clustered around that iconic erotic figure, and how, with precise, controlled poetic movement, H.D. deconstructs both the adoration and the revulsion typical of that process (Friedman, *Psyche Reborn*, pp.232–6).[37]

Thus early in her career, naming, speaking, reading/ decoding, and translating emerge as central activities for the characters about whom H.D. writes, activities which invest erotic energy with discursive desires: first, a desire to make meaning as a woman, in part by, second, the desire to supplant dominant meanings in gender depiction. So, while for H.D., as for many symbolists, natural signs are a language and can be read through, so for H.D. as a female modernist signs and conventions of depiction themselves have lost their naturalised quality and reveal themselves as cooked and brewed, saturated and inspissated with ideologies – of gender, *inter alia*. But finally, her hermetic textual assumptions unveil a nature in which is revealed the feminine/maternal psyche, the metamorphosis and resurrection at the core of 'real' reality, a substratum beneath interpretation, only capable of being hidden or revealed, but not susceptible to change.

> . . . I know, I feel
> the meaning that words hide;
> they are anagrams, cryptograms,
> little boxes, conditioned
> to hatch butterflies . . .
>
> (CP, p.540)

All nature, and all words–both, for H.D., anagram/ cryptograms–have been textualised precisely to avoid any unmediated female place except in final mythic apotheosis. These stances invest the female poet with powers of intuition, knowledge and interpretive skills, indeed, make the woman poet/woman hero a major, necessary reader of the signs concealed in both nature and in words. Indeed, in so far as symbolist poetic strategies have mainly been associated with a sense of *Logos*, or incarnation that is inherently patriarchal, H.D.'s particular version of symbolist rediscovery of an ahistorical ancient verity effects a major cultural displacement by insistently making the matriarchal female power of the mother-goddess figures dominant. Consequently, H.D. has a different approach to the word: language is not really, or exclusively, *Logos*, but can be variously a series of metonymic hatchings from the secret languages of hieroglyph,'anagram and crypto-gram', but can also be a stance beyond language. This latter is especially clear in *Trilogy* II which presents three kinds of wordlessness: a nameless state in which thought is minimised, music, and an empty but readied or incipient book.

H.D.'s love, enthusiasm and capacity for re-animating a past deadened by pedantry flaunted the insouciance and intuitions of poetry back at the 'too gentlemanly, too scholarly, too bloodless' (NEPG, Part II, 'Winter Roses', p.2). Clearly, a critical stance available to a passionate woman opposed to bloodless gentlemen, it is also clearly the voice of a poet contemptuous of 'the small-town attitude of so many of the professional grammarians' (NEPG, Part II, 'Pausanius', p.5). Pound's early criticism and its similar tone, especially his examination of the potent spirit of medieval Latin literature in *The Spirit of Romance* (1910), may well have inspired H.D.'s notes on the potent spirit of classical Greek in these unpublished essays.

To enter the classics is to confront the issue of cultural authority, for knowledge of Greek and Latin, formerly barred to women and certain males, was the sigil of knowledge and authority, the main portal of the liberal humanist hegemony. In the construction of enabling relations between sexuality and textuality, one of the major uses to which H.D. puts the classics is 'battling a valued and loved literary tradition to forge a self out of the materials of otherness', especially traditions of representation (Homans, 1980, p.12).

H.D., quite able to negotiate in classical Greek, assumed its cultural authority in a critical way. She was the mystic against the scholars, she was the woman against male culture, she was the intuitive supporter of all – whether poets, mystics, children singing Euripides' lyrics, or pilgrims – who pierced the word to its spirit.

To strive with her quondam cultural dependency and to solemnify for herself cultural power, H.D. studied and elaborated the written trace of female presence in the major genres of the classical world.[38] Gender and genre studies fuse. She 'engenders' her Greece, treating those poets who were women (Sappho, Nossis, Anyte, Moero, Telesila), those male poets who supported women (Meleager), and those who (for various reasons of assertion and need) H.D. could see as feminine. In this category is the playwright to whom she was most indebted – 'Euripides is a white rose, lyric, feminine, a spirit'.[39] She discussed several of his plays in these essays in her readings in the Greek classics; she translated choruses from *Iphegenia, Bacchae, Hecuba*, and all of *Ion* with interleaved comment, making a moderately intergeneric text. She even wrote on 'his' subject, with his cunning, lacerating ironies in her own *Hippolytus*. Later, she borrowed his anti-Homeric rendition of Helen. He was, for her, a critical figure, cutting against the grain of Greek cultural politics, and he may have been her largest inspiration for a revisionary stance.

The traces of women in epic are treated by shorter poems about Homeric 'heroines' – Circe, Calypso, Thetis, Helen, Cassandra; but her desire to recompose epic does not culminate until the 1950s in *Helen in Egypt* (1961), a writing across the epic tradition in theme, in structure, and even genre while alluding to it with every deconstructive step. And finally, to assume cultural authority as a woman poet, H.D. reworked the beginning of the Western lyric in the Greek Anthology, translating, transposing, rewriting, gleaning, moving into and through the classical lyrics (perforce, but suggestively, those in fragments), but especially those poems written by women, and those written about women. While her Greece is not exclusively, nor militantly female, she attends particularly to erotic and sexual elements, and then to versions of the female in Greek culture. In her treatment of Greece, then, she acts in a feminist manner, often placing woman at the centre of inquiry, and asking about the inscription of gender and the female in traditional culture.

Why emphasise the presence of speaking women at the dawn of written lyric tradition? As countless feminist theorists have reminded us, women's writing begins with a very different relation to silence and speech from most men's: Adrienne Rich, Tillie Olsen, Sandra Gilbert and Susan Gubar, Elaine Showalter, Dale Spender have all elaborated what it might mean to women writers to have a history of not being encouraged to, empowered to – but in fact being enjoined from – speech, analysis and song.

H.D.'s subjects and her methods were chosen so she could open a place for herself in a tradition that may have seemed closed and completed. Indeed, *Bid Me to Live*, a novel set in 1917 and reflecting her early life as a poet, shows how the writer, an H.D. figure, passed from translating the 'hoarded treasures' of the grammarians, to 'divination' of the 'inner words', and finally to writing a new coinage as 'she pushed aside her typewriter [from translations and letters to male mentors] and let her pencil and her notebook take her elsewhere'.[40] 'Elsewhere' was a significant cultural space entered by H.D. with a strong mission, of re-animating significant lyric poets of Greece – especially the women. She thereby offers an interpretive displacement from Greek heroic culture, putting emphasis on neither war nor adventure (central for an epic poet) but on other feelings, other

19

stories. In fact, despite the Virgilian tag (cited as epigraph here) and its unsettling epic implications, H.D. summed up her lyric strategies, in *Paint it To-day*, as the depicting of a special essence of flower, her voice neither feminine (pressing fern fronds) nor scientific (noting every exact detail) but some new fusion and transcendence of those suggestive polarities (PIT, Ch. II, 5).

> Large epic pictures bored her, though she struggled through them. She wanted the songs that cut like a swallow-wing the high, untainted ether, not the tragic legions of set lines that fell like black armies with terrific force and mechanical set action, paralyzing, or broke like a black sea to baffle and to crush. (PIT, Chapter I, 13)

To be anti-epic was to be anti-masculinist and anti-war.

To negotiate the sexual and textual options for herself as a self-consciously female poet, H.D. examines the Hellenic poet and anthologist Meleager (140–70 BC), who is an ideal precursor/mentor precisely because he honours woman writers. Meleager's work is a model of the interpenetration of sexuality and textuality, between women as spoken about and women as speakers, between women as 'girls' (his Heliodora) and women as 'poets' (on his list are Sappho, Nossis, Moero, Anyte, all figures who play some role in H.D.'s early work). His inventive preface to the *Garland* assigned and offered in tribute an imaginatively appropriate flower to each poet.

> *He sought for Moēro, lilies,*
> *and those many,*
> *red-lilies for Anyte,*
> *for Sappho, roses,*
> *with those few, he caught*
> *that breath of the sweet-scented*
> *leaf of iris,*

the myrrh–iris,
to set beside the tablet
and the wax
which Love had burnt,
when scarred across by Nossis:

(Cp, pp. 156–7)

is an embedded citation from Meleager's Preface, as H.D. herself is at pains to note in a few remarks as to sources in *Heliodora*.[41]

This intuitive gesture, implying some hermetic language of flowers, as the 'swallow-wing' implied the task of divination, appealed greatly to H.D. The offering, to each, seems especially to unify the textual and sexual identities of 'girl' and 'poet', for flowers could with equal justice be laid 'upon the altar of love and on the altar of song' (NEPG, Part III, 'Garland', p.5). Further, Meleager was reputed to be bisexual. Offering a mask for her own 'balanced duality' of intellect and emotion, and for her passionate attachments to both sexes, the poet is then especially noted by H.D. for his invention of a spiritual love 'that was to change the whole trend of civilization' which incorporates his even-handed acknowledgement of women (ibid., pp.2, 5). He functions ideologically as an early figure in H.D.'s occult history of humankind.

In both Meleagerian poems by H.D. ('Nossis' and 'Heliodora') a contest or debate takes place between two males.[42] In 'Heliodora', about the woman as muse, two poets strive 'for a name', for words and images sufficient to praise Heliodora, and thereby to make a mark in poetry. If they love well, they will write well. Sexual intensity and textual intensity go together.[43] In 'Nossis', about a woman poet, an auditor tests Meleager by scoffing at that woman's achievement; the poem educates the scoffer to understand both the flower used as tribute and the passionate impact of her work: that

21

her words are so 'warm' that the wax text is sexually aroused by them and softens.

> 'Honey,' you say:
> honey? I say 'I spit
> honey out of my mouth:
> nothing is second-best
> after the sweet of Eros.'
> (CP, p.157)

Note that the Nossis cited is a passage of resistance to conventional tropes praising love; in her critique, Nossis becomes more extravagant in both resistance and evidence of desire.

Meleager's inclusion of women prominently as poets in this early anthology was a gesture vitally important to H.D., for it stated unequivocally that despite the ambiguous and varied political and legal status of ancient women, Greek women lyricists were 'in some subtle way co-workers with men' (ibid., p.7). Meleager thus offered what H.D. was seeking, a constructive model of gender relations in culture which at the same time did not ignore the possibility of a chivalric iconisation of woman–the best, one might argue, of both possible worlds, of both discourses. By teaching our culture that poetic tradition included women writers by an insistent refabrication of their poems, and then by reflecting, as Meleager did, upon their specific 'fragrance', H.D. builds herself a heritage ample enough (and nimble enough) to honour her own cultural – and feminine – presence. By projecting back an interpretive version of Greek gender relations, she justifies her own writing and some of the erotic charge upon which it drew. Hence her use of Greek materials, building both a present and a past, bolsters her own cultural ambitions as a woman writer: to synthesise 'woman' with 'writer', to be both Heliodora and Nossis.

Given her 'avid' and 'naked' interest in engendering the Greek tradition, it is wholly fitting that among H.D.'s boldest lyric works are refabrications of Sappho. The longing for Sappho among all lyric poets can be very intense, but to need Sappho as a literary woman is to participate in an erotic-textual chain of longing that occurs for several reasons, not the least that Sappho has been left in fragments, and hence can be fleshed out, re-animated by being rewritten. Sappho's major appearance in half-line scraps ('parsley shoots'; 'dripping towel') also allows her to be an imagist precursor for her precision, concision and elliptical presentation with (apparently) no unnecessary word or gesture.[44]

Further, the subjects about which Sappho wrote (mother–daughter bonds, strong female friendships, lesbian erotic ties) are often culturally censored. In fact, when H.D. wrote essays about Sappho and Nossis, she noted with particular grief the way they were singled out for destruction by 'the malevolence of the Church. Not, be it noted, of the Christ' (ibid., p.6). The 'ghoulish' monks preserved misogynous satires but destroyed the words of 'these spiritual–emotional Greek women' (ibid., p.6). H.D. refabricates Sappho with fierce purpose in order to salvage a victory over censors of a (literally) patriarchal tradition, then to give voice to a vital but semi-voiceless figure, and finally to attack and disassemble tactics that silence women as cultural producers. H.D. thereby offers herself both foremother and cultural justice in one economic gesture.

For women, Sappho can be the quintessential female precursor. The triple blankness which Sappho offers – the marred text, the lack of female presence in literary history, and the cultural silence about lesbianism – can provoke a triple collaboration: completing a text, creating a 'literary matrilineage' by inventing a female classical inheritance, and finally acknowledging a hidden sexuality.[45]

H.D. saw herself both as a writer in Sappho's tradition and as a Sapphic writer. Her Sappho poems are 'Fragment 113', 'Fragment 36', 'Fragment 40', 'Fragment 41', 'Fragment 68' and 'Calliope'. Certain of the Sappho poems are 'coming out' texts in which H.D. allows herself to name the lesbian aspect of her sexuality. H.D. reserves for Sappho her most special evocativeness, a whiteness, an electric white passion, a star, elsewhere in H.D. indicative of female bonding, articulation of female power, or lesbianism: 'I think of the words of Sappho as these colours, or states rather, transcending colour yet containing (as great heat the compass of the spectrum) all colour' (NTV, p.58). She is, then – as Mary will be in *Trilogy* – whiteness that unifies and transcends a rainbow.

A trio of poems about heterosexual betrayal, infidelity and pain, registered in 1916, at the break-up of her marriage are later revised and transposed into the Sappho poems of 1924, making clear that 'Greece' functioned in an interlocking fashion: as a sign of female cultural authority, and as a set of associations sufficient to encode issues of sexuality.[46] In the shift, male–female love is de-emphasised, and an alternative sexuality is debated, but in both versions, questions of trust and betrayal are paramount. That is, if certain strategic excisions pull the poems away from thraldom to men, especially male sexuality, still the words reposition her in thrall to Aphrodite, who mediates the passion and betrayals. Cutting the celebration of male sexuality and grief about desertion from 'Amaranth' and transposing it to the fabrication in the Sappho 'Fragment 41', with its foot bleeding on a white marble temple; cutting a fervent description of lovemaking including a poetic treatment of ejaculation in 'Eros' to leave a picture of someone shattered by love's bitter-sweetness ('Fragment 40'); transposing 'Envy' to 'Fragment 68', in which the woman envies the man's ability to express his passionate extremism in socially mandated war, all leave poems in which Aphrodite, not any specific male, is H.D.'s antagonist (Martz, CP, p.xxii).

Of two other Sappho projections, 'Fragment 36' and 'Fragment 113', one is a mock-debate between love and poetry, which claims to have the least of both worlds, although encoded acts of passion and poem-making belie her *humilitas* ploy. The other is a strong farewell to tempting predatory physical sexuality in favour of the stronger 'skeleton' behind the flesh, the Platonic essence of Eros – a powerful austere intensity, as strong as sexual drive, but less vulnerable.

'Fragment 36' uses in a powerful and notable way tactics of invention that become distinctive in H.D.'s style. The irregularly placed rhyme (interior rhyme, and rhyme lacking any numerical scheme, assonance), as well as constant alliteration give the binding and connecting advantages of echo with the naturalised voice of *vers libre*.

> I know not what to do:
> strain upon strain,
> sound surging upon sound
> makes my brain blind;
> as a wave-line may wait to fall
> yet (waiting for its falling)
> still the wind may take
> from off its crest,
> white flake upon flake of foam,
> that rises,
> seeming to dart and pulse

and rend the light,
so my mind hesitates
above the passion
quivering yet to break . . .
                    (CP, p.167)

As well, the rhyme and sound practices like alliteration create a looping backward and forward moving and racing–a 'dart and pulse', a phrase H.D. was to use recurrently, always with strong sexual connotations. This racing yet replicative quality is characteristic of H.D.'s voice.

   H.D.'s examination of gender in the classical world led her to construct dramatic monologues reinterpreting myth in the voices of its muted female heroes, deliberate attempts at point of view experiments that could both change narrative sequence and change ideological position. Giving the muted female character her own story postulates that alternative observations and possibly radically different interpretations of central choices and acts can be read from a well-known myth. This shift of narrative paradigm can create a critique of the assumptions and values implied in the hegemonic story.

   Contemporary feminist critics, drawing on the analysis of feminist poets like Adrienne Rich, have identified this revisionary strategy as the critique of dominant culture by the rewriting of dominant narrative. The postulates of these revisionary analyses are as follows: that certain hegemonic stories and images prevail in culture. These androcentric statements tend to read out, disparage or marginalise the meaning of female figures. Yet the narratives, whether secular or sacred, have high status. Despite the existence of muted stories, such as Euripides' not Homer's Helen, the hegemonic stories prevail. Hence to give muted figures a voice within such stories is to break modes of non-speaking and partial telling on which the construction of women as well as stories depend. Women writers become 'thieves of language': in this Hermesian/hermetic act they 'are concerned explicitly with [literary and rhetorical] strategies of overcoming female victimisation and muteness'.[47]

H.D.'s revisionary strategy has been well documented by several feminist critics, each, indeed, illustrating the tactic with a different classicising poem.[48] Susan Friedman discusses the way H.D.'s 'revisionist myth-making' returns the speech of repressed women to culture, and how a specific figure – Callypso – angry, direct, judgemental of men, redefines norms of love and betrayal when telling her story. By changes in perspective and context, H.D. displaces those dominant interpretations which are a form of 'patriarchal desecration' of female figures (Friedman, *Psyche Reborn*, pp.240, 244). Alicia Ostriker shows how H.D. asserts 'the primacy of female experience against traditions that purport to explain it': 'enough of tale, myth, mystery, precedent' H.D. states in 'Demeter' (Ostriker, 1983, p.24).

There are two prongs to this revisionary strategy (DuPlessis, 1985, pp.103–10). In displacement to the 'other side of the story', the writer identifies with otherness and examines the 'taboo, despised, marginalised'. In delegitimation, the writer not only reverses perspective, but realigns narrative elements (motivation, sequence, resolution, cause and effect), rupturing story-as-usual by materials and meanings that dissent 'from social norms as well as narrative forms' (ibid., p. 20). The reinterpretation of female hero/ines is a culturally empowering action for a woman writer who moves this hero/ine into subject place, foregrounding her voice, justifying her choices, making her story emotionally and politically plausible. H.D.'s early revisionary poems, few though they are, contain the seeds for later massive and magisterial retellings in *Trilogy* and *Helen in Egypt*.

Yet H.D. would never be satisfied with a confrontative or purely oppositional stance. Thus her use of mythic narrative can be summed up in the mysterious motto 'the same – different – the same attributes,/ different yet the same as before' from *Trilogy* (CP, p.571). A good deal of H.D.'s reading and poetic scholarship (as in *By Avon River*, in her scholarly novels about the Rossetti circle in her final period, and in the whole encounter with Freud) goes towards the establishment of a secret understanding of the truth really concealed in an occulted substratum of human and cultural experience. For example, her truth of the mother, once emergent, is both different – culturally unacknowledged – and yet the same: forgotten, buried but never original (new) or invented. It is only original by being origins. Despite her gender critique and her narrative and linguistic innovations, H.D. felt the new did not really exist. Thus, perhaps, the shock to her system whenever technological terror – certain deadly forms arguably new – (the sinking of the Lusitania, the bombing of London, the atomic bomb) made active, raw wounds. She resolved this conflict by offering herself as the medium whereby such events were reassimilated to bygone patterns and mythic narrative.

In Greece, H.D. sought social, cultural, religious marginalities (Meleager as 'Hellenic Jew'); critique (Euripides as 'anti-social', an 'iconoclast' and, importantly, an 'anti-war' outsider) (NEPG, Part I, 'Euripides', p.2); the trace of a lost culture (an essay on Messenia, loser in combat with Sparta); and the trace of the female which interlocked with all other kinds of difference.

Most significant about all the marginals is their loyalty to remember the almost lost, as the Messenians remembered their rites, language and customs after years of exile. This devotion to the muted becomes a model for an exiled élite of palimpsesters, loyal to a partly eradicated vision despite their being temporally and culturally scattered with the objects of their regard broken into fragments. There is no doubt that a nostalgia for wholeness and presence animates much of H.D.'s work.

Hymen (1921), a masque, is a static and weighted attempt to (re)create a woman's ritual, including all kinds of males but mature, sexually active ones. The anthropological desire, however commendable, is not lively in the first place, and the frieze-like offerings of various ages and types of women, and of Eros himself, are rich and elaborate, but overdrawn. However, the masque also shows an enormous desire to recreate that part of the culture of ancient Greece which is least known because not recorded in the same way that epic records the wars of heroes. In that sense, *Hymen* continues a female-centred project of the revisionary recovery of stories which comes to most overwhelming fruition in *Helen in Egypt*. The sequence also shows a critical negotiation with some of the love lyrics typical of the Greek Anthology – individual songs of seduction or praise, charming woman. Instead, the lyrics of *Hymen* form a carefully mapped ritual of passage, for and by a community of women, through female life-stages in which love is holy. In short, the offering is dedicatory, not amatory or seductive.

A curious early poem of H.D.'s husband, Richard Aldington, might alert us to some of the stakes H.D. felt in her loyalty to the ancient world throughout her career.[49]

Hermes and Thoth and Christ are rotten now,
Rotten and dank . . .
And through it all I see your pale Greek face;
Tenderness
Makes me as eager as a little child to love you,
You morsel left half-cold on Caesar's plate.

One might see H.D.'s aim in her career as a whole, to reverse and relentlessly reassess the spiritual and sexual assumptions in this interesting set of lines, which were doubtless addressed to her. A woman is here asked to be ideological and sexual compensation for the major changes in Western civilisation that the poem also implies she has somehow missed. 'Half-cold' can refer to his version of her sexuality or to the leftover world view in which her 'Greekness' – not to speak of that array of gods – becomes stale, pale and dank. H.D. seeks to prove that these gods are not dead – indeed, these precise gods and more will animate *Trilogy* – and rotten but perpetually resurrected. Aldington postulates that this woman needs him to cushion shocks at the loss of ancient verity. The 'morsel' herself, in her career, seeks to invent a dynamic and even erotic relationship with the spiritual depths of an animated ancient world, especially with Great Mother goddesses thereby denying this poem's major premise – that the gods are dead – as well as its minor one that wistful romance is compensatory for this loss. Rather, as H.D. will argue, Eros is a special case of spiritual animation.

Chapter Two

The Authority of 'Otherness'

A lady will be set back in the sky. It will be no longer
Arcturus and Vega but stray star-spume, star sprinkling
from a wild river, it will be myth; mythopoeic mind (mine)
will disprove science and biological–mathematical definition.

(HERmione (1927), p.76)

By a tremendous output of prose fiction, H.D. extended
her range and challenged her continuing 'canonisation'
as imagist saint (miracle worker and icon) which had
been solemnified in a young *Collected Poems* in 1925, only
twelve years after her first publication as H.D.[1] In this
second period alone (1920/25–1933/34), there are three
groups of novels: a *Magna Graeca* set (*Hedylus* and
Palimpsest); the 'Madrigal cycle' (*Paint it To-day, Asphodel,
HERmione*, and the later *Bid Me To Live (A Madrigal)*); and a
Borderline group.[2]
  One project of this prose is to unify such female
experiences as (lesbian, bisexual, heterosexual) sexuality
and motherhood with creative power. H.D. struggles to

assume the authority of Otherness so that female-centred experiences and ties are the source of theme and character, narrative and resolution, language and rhythm. This is not achieved without a struggle with negative evaluations of female situations, especially the mother–daughter tie, but also the trustworthiness of some lesbian relations. A related project of H.D.'s prose is to elide the Otherness of women with the otherness of both visionary and artist. So many of the novels – certainly the three discussed here – offer the overlapping stories of *Bildungs-* and self-reflexive *Kunstlerroman* about the repeated formations of a woman artist who must 'create her creativity' given the social, psychic, ideological and political events reverberating with her femaleness: the conditions in which she writes as a woman, the politics of gender (Jehlen, 1981, p.583). H.D. begins to claim herself in Otherness by ceasing to be the perfect poet and becoming–something else; writing, as Mary Jacobus has tersely indicated, 'elsewhere, elsehow' (Abel (ed.), *Writing and Sexual Difference*, p.38).

Because the issue of escaping possession by others included her contrary tendency towards hypocathexis to an ideal (poetry or vision) in the form of a desired object (D.H. Lawrence, say, among others) that is so intensely illustrated in a number of her relationships, and because such an escape from possession included as well the risk of naming and engaging with self-possession, it is not surprising that another kind of possession becomes, and remains, a life-long issue. At the time when her friendships with Lawrence and Pound and her marriage to Aldington were ending, at the time when she had just given difficult birth to a child whose patrimony led to complicated crises, at a time when H.D. and Bryher had struck up their love *cum* friendship (what was to be a life-long allegiance), H.D. experienced a cluster of visionary experiences (in the early 1920s) whose appropriate use became a major task of her poetic career. That is, as she attempts to exit from the poetic and romantic thraldoms of her early career, intent on her successful maternity and her bond with Bryher, she experiences a special haunting kind of possession by a 'writing on the wall' and other experiences which made her feel chosen, gifted – and frightened. Especially notable is the Corfu vision in which Bryher participated, and in whose mysterious object-symbols (soldier, goblet, tripod, Niké, sun-disc), like a veiled autobiography both after the fact and before one could apparently find scripts for life, for poetry, for 'the questions that have been asked through the ages, that the ages will go on asking'; if only they could be properly decoded (TF, p.55). The otherness of these psychic events collects and thickens H.D.'s general interest in the movement of the mind through 'memories, visions, dreams, reveries' by attention to a peculiar but incontrovertible real event 'in thought, in imagination, or in the realm of memory' (TF, p.35). This is a potent form of otherness which accompanies and intensifies female Otherness.

A passage purporting to discuss the poet Lo-fu in her notable statement on poetics, *Notes on Thought and Vision* (1919) shows how the 'imagist' tactic of seeing was for H.D. grounded in, or quickly passed into, a meditative visionary practice. 'Imagism' may thus never have been imagism for H.D.; it was always more mystical, suggestive, ineffable. From that perspective, if literary history had already been written by women, one might have heard that, much later than H.D. and possibly under her influence, male poets like Lawrence, Eliot, even Pound realised that mystical vision was the true heart of modernist poetic practice: An excusable feminist wryness.

By claiming these kinds of otherness, H.D. risks being 'perhaps less perfect' and more vulnerable than both her critics and her friends desired. Wonderfully, a debate centres on her new choice of genre: some people were genuinely distressed by her commitment to prose. Her husband Aldington wrote to H.D.; 'Prose? No! You have so precise, so wonderful an instrument – why abandon it to fashion another perhaps less perfect. You have, I think, either to choose pure song or else drama or else Mallarmian subtlety. Which will you choose?'[3] Gender and genre thus intersect at the point of reception as well as at the point of production. Aldington speaks as if he could mastermind her choices, define her options, and thus own her successes; certainly such a letter allows him to disown her failures. H.D. understands the debate is about the possession of her own literary identity: not a speaking subject only, she has also been a producing object in whom others had made a certain investment. Thus with a dour amusement upon the publication of part of *Palimpsest* 'which I like but people don't think "worthy" quite of H.D. . . . I say WHO is H.D.? They all think they know more about what and why she should or should not be or do than I.'[4] The 'she' who is 'I' would claim for 'I' all the otherness of 'she'.

What does it mean to claim Otherness? In H.D.'s terms, it is to claim 'Her' (H.D.'s title for an important novel)–the subject claims its dominated, object case for scrutiny, claims the uncontained self, claims her visions, claims the lesbian/bisexual, claims maternity at both ends, as mother and as daughter. During the second part of her career, H.D. entered into a series of debates with her own Otherness, asking how to represent and explore its distinctive elements in writing.

Now the idea of Otherness, applied to women, has had a long history as a major framework of Western thought. The static, defining condition of woman as ideal (magical symbol of wholeness) and/or monster (mistress of the carnal and the contingent) is based mainly, as Dorothy Dinnerstein has clarified, on women's physical tasks in reproduction and the care in woman-maintained motherhood. Simone de Beauvoir foregrounded the staggering heritage in a book both analysis, polemic and elegy: female Otherness in the form of bondage to immanent tasks of repetitive care impeded women's joining history, blocked women's risk-taking situational (existentialist) choices, foreclosed women's participating in the reciprocal dialectics of self and other.[5]

De Beauvoir's powerful summary of this absolutist position shows that through the socially maintained introjection of this major image of Otherness, both men and women escape fully authentic life. In order to get to a stage of human/historical evolution in which both genders may act in conditions of choice, the problematic of woman (at least) must be faced and solved by both ideological and structural change, not the smallest of which is the rupture of dualisms which are moreover situated strongly and suggestively in gender itself. Both men and women must critically read gender. And since the writings of the eighteenth century, women have often been caught (as in the museum scene of *Villette*) reading the codes and depictions of this 'Woman' that has such claims on their attention.

At the same time that there is a dominant literary and philosophic tradition about female Otherness, there is also a strong social, historical (and sometimes ideological) position concerning women as historical actors striving to achieve civil rights. The debate between 'difference' (female Otherness) and 'rights' (female 'sameness' or perfect equality) has in fact characterised feminism. These historical struggles for educational access, for fair laws governing divorce, property and control of sexual reproduction, for work for middle-class women, for the vote, were still lively enough in H.D.'s era, reflected by her in a jealous moment in *HERmione* in which she yearns, given the accomplishments of one woman pianist, to achieve something herself, in a bravura attempt at a 'New Woman's' life in Greenwich Village (1910), and in one unpublished story concerning female suffrage. So while H.D. (as all of us) profited from 'rights' feminism, she was extremely drawn to the feminism of 'difference.'

One might say that a woman writer must necessarily attempt to achieve an attitude to the idea of female Otherness, if only because, as Gilbert and Gubar have eloquently shown in *The Madwoman in the Attic*, it may impede or impound her very writing career itself. Certainly no woman can claim complete exemption from being affected by both the negative, debilitating and positive, tempting aspects of that Otherness, including (as Adrienne Rich's 'Snapshots of a Daughter-in-Law' indicates) some astonishing double binds. Nor can one achieve anything – writing, say – while completely conniving in, complicit with, the limits of that Otherness. Therefore, however illogical the contradictions or however unstable the compound, women have consistently attempted to unite the two aims: 'How can the double demand – for both equality and difference – be articulated?' This move is, of course, undualistic in implication.[6]

This 'double demand' has had a great influence on the work of a number of women writers, H.D. included, and it is positioned in their texts in a number of ways. The 'double demand' occurs in Virginia Woolf's *A Room of One's Own* in a muted debate between the dark 'serpentine caves' of otherness/difference (suggesting in context lesbianism, female bonding, motherhood, and the physicality of vaginal and uterine sites), and the incandescent, mental flash of androgyny, or coequality between a male and female half.[7] In a similar vein, H.D. debated difference and equality in two statements from the early 1920s which embolden her in her project of writing Otherness, and to which I shall momentarily return.

The positions in question might themselves be in debate in one period of a writer's life: in the previous chapter, one could see H.D. minimising difference when she speaks of men and women as coequal cultural workers, yet maximising it with her irregular appeals to female iconisation. In the period under scrutiny here, a heady entrance into her own 'lesbian existence' with loyal, intent Bryher, and a relatively protected motherhood after the enormous trauma of Perdita's birth (there were servants, trips without the baby, money, buffers to constant child care) led H.D. to explore Otherness.[8]

Yet as certain contemporary theory postulates, if the other is truly Other (site of the repressed, of the unconscious), it will be virtually inaccessible in normal dominant discourse. This Otherness can never 'truly' be spoken. (One might then ask who knows the 'rules' of this ineffable Otherness so well as to be the arbiter of how, how not, or whether it can be evoked?) This position is accompanied by something like this syllogism: first, 'Other' is a feminine space, based on clichés of the feminine as a dark, unknowable continent. Second, there is a strong coincidence between women and the feminine, and therefore a congruence between Woman and Other. Thus the positing of female Otherness virtually denies speech to women, since even we cannot speak our own Otherness, but because we are Other, we have no other subject. There is something mystically pleasing about positing an ineffable writing, never to be articulated and always beyond, but only as a spur to writing, not as a statement of the absolute or definitional impossibility of speaking and being heard. However, if this idea is accompanied by some invitation to non-dominant discursive practices (as in Hélène Cixous's 'Medusa' manifesto, in Julia Kristeva's 'semiotic chora' or in Luce Irigaray's fluid and passionate essays) the spark of possibility rather than the law of the forbidden prevails. 'A lady will be set back in the sky.'

H.D., always, posited a speaking Otherness, not a silent one, even in the blank book of the new in *Trilogy*. How does she achieve some access to this Other? How does she articulate the double demand for Otherness and equality? First, critically. In this phase of her work, she often speaks about her removal from the status of muse, or merely decorative other, and the critique of romance comes into certain of her novels. Second, relationally. Positing the relational elements of difference that need depiction, she proceeds in a quite definite fashion to portray female sexuality and desire. This is joined by something harder to prove, an approach to otherness via language, in the texture of prose perhaps because it was not held to a monolithic speaking subject – strategies of discourse also associated with avant-garde practice. Irigaray suggests 'parler femme': the phrase contains two essential connotations: to 'speak (as) woman' (the thematic strategies) and to 'speak female' the hint of, the interest in, language practices.

Irigaray [and this can sum up H.D.'s position as well] says repeatedly that there is no one female language. The new speech that she valorizes must explore itself, its selves, in multiple tones and voices. Her text is a process of discovery

and an exploration, through language, of the connections between female sexuality and the expression of
meaning . . . [9]

To speak Otherness meant a special commitment to
speak of sexuality.

In her early work, H.D. had plumbed models of
coequality. In two closely linked texts, she makes a
transition that marks her work in the 1920s: to the
exploration of female difference or Otherness. In 'Helios
and Athene' (1920), a series of anti-imagist wisdom
epigrams on the erotic and spiritual meanings of statues
which also called for 'a new approach to Hellenic
literature and art', H.D. postulates that male and female
gods exist in what her ex-friend D.H. Lawrence was to
call 'star equilibrium', neither conquered by the other
(CP, p.328). At the same time, she formulates the
problem of female Otherness that she sets about to
solve.[10] Athene, the goddess, is double: 'doubly passionate' possessing both 'the softness and tenderness of the
mother and the creative power and passion of the male'
(CP, p.330). Niké 'is the symbol of this double conquest
and double power' (ibid.). This female goddess has
maternal power–Elusinian, as the Demeterian 'guardian
of children' – and has the Apollonian 'very essential male
power' (ibid.). So procreativity and creativity can merge.
A woman can imagine herself writing by seeing herself
as a virgin with maternal power, in the mother–child
dyad, who also has access to male power in her person.
H.D. is imagining the possibility of speech from the
'phallic mother', or mother of power. But to write from
Otherness implies certain more radical, problematic
claims: that a woman's physical experience, her body
itself, allows her access to special spiritual and intellectual insights.

Notes on Thought and Vision (1919/1982 pub.), one of H.D.'s few statements on poetics, functions as a bridge between the Greek poems of passion and cultural quest and the investigation of female Otherness. While on the one hand, *Notes* concerns a conjoined male and female élite, on the other, female ways of knowing through the female body are privileged access points for transformative vision. Sexual energy (the love brain) and psychic understanding (the overbrain) are 'capable of' a special form of thought or 'vision' (NTV, p.22). She argues in an apocalyptic tone reminiscent of both Pound's *obiter dicta* and Lawrence's natural mysticism, that a small élite who received these messages 'could turn the whole tide of human thought, could direct lightning flashes of electric power to slash across, and destroy the world of dead, murky thought' (ibid., p.27).[11] Certain exceptional people (among whom she numbered herself) could function as receiver/transmitters, especially for ancient materials (both Greek and Christian) – statues, images, texts. And lovers who are initiates through the physical body to a spiritual Eros constitute this élite. H.D. begins here to particularise what becomes a central motif of her *oeuvre*: the spiritual meaning of erotic passion.

At the same time that the *Notes* concentrate on the quest that male and female seekers have in common, H.D. also asks, 'Is it easier for a woman to attain this state of consciousness than for a man?' and 'Should we [women] be able to think with the womb and feel with the brain?' (NTV, p.20). The questions are bold and tentative at once, excited by yet resistant to that postulate of female difference. But H.D. does here declare the advantages of female physicality, of female Otherness on the vision quest which remained the highest aspiration for both genders. And, in so doing, she 'rewrites conventional phallic metaphors for creativity' (Morris, 1984, p.419). 'I first realised this state of consciousness in my head. I visualise it just as well, now, centred in the love-region of the body or placed like a foetus in the body' (NTV, p.19). So she argues in a Tiresean fashion that the female body in its physical presence has a special gift: dual lenses for vision. Together, womb and mind 'bring the world of vision into consciousness' (ibid., p.23).

H.D.'s two lenses of brain and womb may be responses to the two lenses each of her 'fathers' controlled: the telescope of an astronomer father and the microscope of her biologist grandfather, both of whom had written standard works of 'biological–mathematical definition' in the course of their lives. Note the importance to H.D. of disproving this male way of thinking, of striking a fire from Helios with some female lens, equalling what her Promethean brother did once as a child, stealing a magnifying glass from their father's desk to strike a flame from the sun (TF, pp.21–7). She claimed her visionary space of female Otherness in struggle with already existing, mightily-gendered family patterns of authority, of rational explanation, and of male-to-male succession. In defiance, she offers her image for the unconscious: two 'jellyfish' lenses, like amniotic fluid or, returning abruptly to the two-sexed metaphors, like sperm and egg, to nurture and contain a mysterious kind of thinking. This 'thinking' conforms to H.D.'s basic trinity of mother, father and very special child: *Notes on Thought and Vision* ends by a return to the two sexes and their creation – a mysterious child who is beyond gender (like Christ). But the work passes through a serious consideration of the knowledge to be achieved from the female body, from female difference. The attempt to postulate an overlayered centre of authority in female and mystical otherness is evident.

Contemporary critical writing on the female *Kunstler-roman* agrees that women's growth into the creative act, as depicted by women, is tied emotionally and materially with issues of the maternal, with procreativity, and with identification with women ranging from resistance to merging. Susan Gubar has proposed that the 'centrality of childbearing' in women's 'artist novels' ruptures a controlling historical and ideological either/or choice for women of either creation or procreation; she suggests that with this merging of creativity and procreativity 'feminist modernists struggled against the conservative consequences of asserting a natural and distinct sphere'. In *Writing Beyond the Ending*, I analysed the shift from nineteenth to twentieth-century women's *Kunstlerromane* as the displacement of a thwarted woman in a heterosexual plot to an emergent daughter in a re-parenting plot, where the daughter-artist extends and completes, in cross-generational collaboration, the unfinished artisanal work of her parent. Bell Chevigny's discussion of the bond of a woman scholar with her female subject argues that the scholar enacts a personal and pre-Oedipal subtext involving a dialectical identification, symbiosis, mirroring and then differentiation with the subject about whom she writes, who becomes temporarily a 'surrogate mother'. Hélène Cixous's astonishing manifesto 'Laugh of the Medusa' may also be entered as evidence that, far from ideas of female 'lack', the generative m/other, the female body, 'vatic bisexuality', are mighty sources for female creativity.[12]

H.D.'s work offers much evidence for these theses that centre on the maternal spur to creativity. For instance, H.D. knew her mother's 'art' (singing and painting) were in one case repressed by a cruel glancing remark from her own father, and in the other case, set aside. Handcrafts she had made were 'banished' and then 'discarded' (TF, pp.150-1). Yet the sight of her mother's hand-painted dishes 'fire[d] my very entrails with adoration'–a strong proto-sexual metaphor (ibid., p. 151).

The *Magna Graeca* novels discover that one needs the greater force of *Magna Mater*. Taken as a unit, the passage from *Hedylus* (1926/1928 pub.), to *Palimpsest* (1926) marks a mannered struggle with this insight. The gender dramas of *Hedylus*, while self-reflexive, split the creative and the maternal-feminine. Both characters and setting are 'a mythic representation for a state of mind', filled with 'displacements, distortions' and 'doublings' of people and events that marked H.D. (Friedman, *Hedylus* review, Ts., 4, 5). Two deeply locked 'H' characters (mother and son) search for the proper 'D' among three men (Demetrius, Douris, Daimon). Only that 'D' will be able effectively to rupture the paralysing symbiotic compact of the gifted, split boy and the witty hetera, his mother.

Hedyle is an exiled Athenian beauty who has had an illegitimate son, Hedylus, now a tormented poet whose search for his father dominates the book. Both the pre-Oedipal bond and the Oedipal triangle are reconstituted in the prose (longing, belated speeches of both Hedylus and Hedyle to absent father/lover) only to splinter in the event, as the son abandons his mother to take on a destiny linked to the father, who arrives precisely like an hallucination. Until the son can separate, differentiate, rename himself, he is blighted. His identity, his sexuality, his name, his will all are enveloped by hers.[13] Given her later memoir *The Gift*, with its familial female tradition of vision, it is notable that H.D. uses a boyish cover character for what is plausibly seen as a female poet and here represses maternal creativity replacing it with Hedyle's mirrors, her lapis bracelet, and fading beauty.

The work can be read as an Oedipal fable, yet it has a wiry subtext of persistent matrisexuality. H.D. asserts thematically that mother and son have achieved separation: mother acknowledges a former romance, son his desire for a paternal patron. But the work is still about the secret mother, the secret desires for mother, the secrets of mothering, the secret 'birth canal' of Hedylus's hidden place between sea and land, and (yet) the apparent necessity for the paternal 'phallus' to enter this place and make it healthy, instead of self-absorbed, stifling. But H.D.'s structure erases that thematic point and makes the novel a study in maternal–filial envelopment and ambivalence, in part because of the notable suffocation of the style.

The playful, deadly, persistent use of her own initials is difficult to decode except as they flaunt the autobiographical, the admission of personal necessities into the heart of the work. It is clear that the 'H' and the 'D' represented different, difficultly reconciled needs: say, for intensity and for nurturance. Since H.D. and the letters 'h' and 'd' are equally present in Hedyle/mère and Hedylus/fils, is she postulating that her maternity and her poetry are split, that her maternity challenges and suffocates her intensity, her vision, her poetry? Since Hedylus's girlfriend is also a clear version of Bryher, the lesbian is encoded, and there may be a depiction of the split between heterosexual and homosexual sides of the self. Friedman succinctly summarises the exposures and encodings:

> One persona [Hedyle] embodies H.D.'s heterosexual self, identified as female; the other [Hedylus] encodes the lesbian self, projected into a male body. One is the woman. The other is the poet. The split self, doubled into two characters, seems irrevocable. (Friedman, review of *Hedylus*, Ts.7)

In the terms I have proposed here, her different 'othernesses' (lesbianism, maternity, vision) are all colliding. There are still other possibilities. Her maternity and her poetry may be found alike dependent on her deeply repressed pre-Oedipal yearnings for a mother. The novel is as schematic as its interpretations.

Besides playing with the splits and dilemmas of female authorship, this work, begun in the year her *Collected Poems* was published, marks the beginning of her incessant assessment of her achievement as an 'imagist'. Her imagist poems are encoded in the novel as Hedylus, the character, 'the portrait or projection of the intellectualised crystalline youth', a precise symbol of the limits of her 'crystalline' poetry.[14] Here begins a major interior drama and challenge H.D. posed to herself: how to achieve a 'crystal' work in which there is also 'fire.'

Palimpsest is a *Kunstlerroman* of three overlayered stories, from different eras, situating female protagonists at sequent points in an aesthetic and spiritual quest: choosing to be a writer, choosing to remain a writer, and choosing to seek what lies beyond or beneath the merely creative. This work too was, as Susan Friedman has said of all H.D.'s fiction, another attempt 'to retell, reorder and thereby recreate her own "legend" ' (Friedman, *Dictionary of Literary Biography*, Ts. p.36). In each section, the main character's inner allegiance shifts from romance and men to female bonding and maternal yearning, even when, as in 'Hipparchia', the mother was originally viewed with distaste, or, as in 'Murex', when the female eventually identified with was once a bitter sexual rival. Or, even as in 'Secret Name', when a reverberating sexual attraction to a mysterious stranger seems controlling. In all cases, there is some desire plumbed, which results in three related passages of mirroring: bonding with female Otherness seals the woman in her vocation as a writer – a very different solution from that proposed in *Hedylus*, in which creativity was overtly coded as male: male poet, and the male inspiration of father-muse. The three 'prose studies' (NRW, pp.9/10) comprising *Palimpsest* are also part of the *Magna Graeca* set, in which antiquity functions as a political and psychological trope: its political terms a relation to colonisation and a challenge to the false authority of conquest alone; its psychological terms, the discovery by archaeology of the deepest stratum of origins. Both valences have a clear gender import, and both involve the quest for value.

In 'Hipparchia', the female hero/ine, an elegant Greek woman is sleeping with the enemy – two types of Roman conqueror, both soldier and aesthete (shades of Aldington and Cecil Gray). Hipparchia represents Greece which she is certain 'is now lost' – politically, morally, aesthetically. The young Bryeresque Roman girl she meets at the end of the story is the first hint that her dramatic, culturally transformative ambition might be realised: 'Greece is a spirit. Greece is not lost' (P, p.94). These lines from her own poetry inspired Julia to seek Hipparchia's friendship and can re-inspire Hipparchia to her vocation.[15]

All Hipparchia's activity, all her writing, will be a purposeful charm 'eventually to destroy Rome', for the conquering civilisation had to 'die, spiritually influenced by Athens' (ibid., p.73). So 'Hipparchia' first concerns colonial relations and subversions in which a courtesan of colonised Corinth finds in herself the means of beginning the historical task of rupturing Roman hegemony by strategic use of the very cultural 'plunder' (herself included) by which Romans were fascinated (ibid., p.74). She will undo, by her web of words and her books mixing science, poetry and ethics, the Roman conquest which all take as utterly triumphant. She is inspired to this project by Julia's faithful affection and by overcoming her ambivalent distaste for her mother, also a famous poet, which signals the end of her illness and of her courtesan's languid spitefulness. She is able to claim oracular knowledge coterminus with maternal vision.

Hipparchia thus exactly replicates an earlier decision made by the first Hipparchia, her mother, to reject the feminine, for her intellectual and poetic vocation, yet this vocation, as her mother enacted it implied a heterosexual identification with men. What H.D. tells herself again and again, by means of *Palimpsest*, is that there is a rich thematic, stylistic, emotional and intellectual area in the longing for women, an area whose dimensions she must explore. Creativity comes in the identification with Otherness. But there is difficult terrain to traverse before this identification can be made. This too is narrated here. Because Hipparchia feels abandoned, tested and 'plagued' by her mother, she resists the writer's vocation which they share (P, p.78). In a striking reading of this material, Deborah Kelly Kloepfer traces the narrative movement from resistance and hostility to the maternal, through a success with a translation (of a woman poet, Moero), followed by a hallucinating torment by the spirit of the mother and a delirium of illness in the daughter. 'The mother is inscribed variously as absence, as Isis, as artistic denial, as muse, as severance, as integration. . . .'[16]

Merging and self-identification are indicated stylistically, with the interplay of name and of choice indicated in a triple verbal palimpsest: 'Hipparchia would protect Hipparchia from Hipparchia' (P, p.78). That is, the mother as poet protects the gifted daughter from her

temptation into courtesanship. And as well, the daughter
-writer protects herself from the destructive mother by
her fusion of feminine crafts (embroidery and weaving)
with her mother's more austere rejection of 'women
seated at the distaff,/ weighted with silk and ornament!'
(ibid., p.8). The drama is completed when Julia's
admiration and sisterly care also support Hipparchia's
vocation. These are significant narrative moments of
identification with and exploration of maternal and
sororal figures, for through them (and not through the
somewhat disinterested sex, earlier in the story)
narrative climax and emotional meaning are created.
This research into the authority of Otherness drains the
heterosexual plot of its meaning, and establishes the
search for female power as a goal of narrative.

In 'Murex', the second palimpsest, Raymonde
Ransome, a blocked writer, is living a time-warp of ten
years (1916–26) in post-war London, resisting her own
vocation by resisting both grief and forgiveness. Her
'repudiat[ion of] her genius' is related to her painful past,
romantic betrayal, loss of a child, post-war despair, all of
which bubble (and babble) up in the writing in 'layers and
layers of interweaving thought' (P, pp.150,165). This
section's jazzy, obsessive, modern rhythm, the repeated
'feet, feet, feet', indicates easily an urban wasteland, the
soldiers marching off to war and, finally, metre itself,
and the despaired-of vocation as a poet. The hero/ine
feels a split of identity between her vulnerable, feminine
side and her 'other', helmeted Ray Bart, whose gender-
ambiguous name and pressure of inspiration are taxing
reminders of her poetry. Further, she is reluctant even
to feel inspired, in a panic that the men upon whom she
counted as companions in poetry were somehow
unmanned during the war (if they returned at all) and
could no longer perform promising cultural work.

Because it is said that she alone must fulfil their promise as well as hers, Raymonde's fear of poetry is a depression related to survivor's guilt, and possibly a response to this punishing yet seductive agenda of replacement.

'James Joyce was right', she says numerous times, a repentend in the context of a meditation on writing, on Jews, Christians, on immutable law, on modernism, on Greeks and Egyptians, on the ancient world and the post-World War I world, on stillbirth and her ex-husband, offering a licence to mix and mingle a range of materials from the domestic to the mythic. 'Joyce's rightness' appears again to foreground 'laws held inviolate over the merest dust heap. Laws like reading tea-leaves. James Joyce was right. Inflexible laws were to be read in the meanest actions, the set of a ribbon (nowadays one didn't wear ribbons)' (P, p.151). Decoding involves the foregrounding of the tiny meaningful detail, its perusal and understanding. There is a world, in the tiny – a feminist revamping of sentimental 'world in a grain of sand' consolations; there are grave symbolic messages in tealeaves (despite shades of *ersatz* gypsies in tearooms, even shades of Mme Sosostris). And the ribbons, present or absent, recall Virginia Woolf's contemporaneous feminist poetics: especially its transvaluation of 'trivial' and 'important'. The female sensibility had a special calling. It ranged 'among almost unknown or unrecorded things; it lighted on small things and showed that perhaps they were not small after all'.[17] The contrast of the ironically important 'battlefield' with the ironically insignificant clothes shopping is another of Woolf's beribboned tropes (Woolf, *AROO*, p.77). There was a new aesthetic sought here – of otherness, of Gestalt shifting from the tiny to the momentous. To bolster her insight into the meanings of this other side, the authority of Joyce is evoked, not (and never) Woolf.[18] It is revealing of H.D.'s felt gender authority to see her depicting a female writer seeking the authority of a male writer for what has latterly been called *'écriture feminine'*.[19]

Because art 'had lost – had lost – its savour . . . must get back into art the magic it had had in Egypt, Greece even. Odd line in Egypt spelt exact and scientific formula' (P, p.155). Formula is an interesting word for H.D. to have chosen; she seems to have meant its connotation of exact, scientific, immutable and mathematically proven law, that answer to paternal authorities by which myth becomes the new science. She assumes the ultimate modernist trope to bolster female Otherness: 'the room eternally the same, and thousands of years and interspersing civilizations but the arm chair the same and the note book. . . ' (P, p.169). That is, by knowledge of eternal recurrence, specific pain can be dissolved, ennobled, emboldened; by an understanding that all people were symbols or abstractions (the specific vamp is a Siren, is Helen), true dramas are uncovered (ibid., p.170). H.D. has discovered her 'mythic method', one she was to extend after the experience of psychoanalysis: daily life was not trivial, but eternal: 'not of to-day, not even of yesterday, but of always and forever' (ibid., p.126).

The confession of Raymonde's young visitor, Ermy, the parallel of her own sexual betrayal even to the identity of the vamp, pierces ten years of self-denial and repression. She and Ermy are 'palimpsested'; even more interestingly, Ermy comes as an overlay of an even further past. 'In the light of her discovery that a just unearthed Egyptian [that is, Ermy] sat there . . . all her values altered' (ibid., p.126). So 'antiquity was security. Laws were immutable' (ibid., p.159). Egypt and Greece, hello, and hello, Rome.

The modernist overlays of palimpsested time reveal one unrelative, immutable truth. 'All of modernity (as she [Ray Bart] viewed it) was as the jellified and sickly substance of a collection of old colourless photographic negatives through which gleamed the reality, the truth of the blue temples of Thebes, of the white colonnades of Samos' (ibid., p.158). Modern times are simply the wobbling, distorting transparencies through which one can still grasp 'inexorable' or 'immutable' laws.

Finding the deeper laws meant – one of the larger Anglo-American modernist hopes – change without political struggle. Change organically (not dialectically) occurring, occurring by conversion. We live among palimpsests of ages, but a final truth glistens at the bottom of all that overscribbled sheet. It is a 'buried, lost, forgotten' – but already constituted – 'treasure' (ibid., p. 179). The final truth for H.D. is the historical and psychological presence of a maternal power, the temple to the mother goddess underneath, and the core of, the paternal erections that post-date it.

Here, too, the main character's inner allegiance shifts from romance and men to female bonding and maternal yearning, even when distaste and bitterness, rejection and repulsion had first marked the character's relation with women. Raymonde's new poem, worked on at length in the section, is inspired by a mirroring moment among three women, one of whom is her double and the other is her 'enemy'. The pronouns clot and the intensity of revulsion turns to loving acceptance. Bonding with female Otherness here as in 'Hipparchia' seals the protagonist in her vocation as a writer. H.D. composes remarkable passages of mirroring and positive envelopment to break the hegemony of the 'Oedipal' plot of romance and transference by attention to the 'pre-Oedipal' plot of fusion, and as she would say later in

51

Tribute to Freud, 'transfusion' (TF, p.151). Indeed, mirroring is a special form of palimpsest in which two separate selves exchange views and each Otherness is seen with the eyes of empathetic identification; in this event break mirrors (remember Hedyle) of beauty and/as that silence in which women in narratives have traditionally languished. The trope of mirroring for female bonding, itself mirrored in the reversing syntax of the passage also occurs, incidentally, in Elizabeth Barrett Browning's *Aurora Leigh* (Sixth Book, 11. 478–506).

Palimpsest presents, in its semi-dissonant third part, out of Greece/Rome/London and into Egypt, not the resolution of a vocation to poetry but the problematic of poetic origins in new kinds of desire. The 'trinkets', the little images from archaeological digs which Rafton offers to Helen, must not be touched as offered, via romance, as signs of seduction, but rather as clues to vast territories of consciousness, a whole buried life of mind with manifold forms of memory, desire, 'depths' not yet visible.

Helen learns that her primary longing is not for romance despite her palpable sexual desire but for study of poetic/mythic origins and meanings, here presented as archaeology, but which clearly also implicate psychology in passages that prefigure *Tribute to Freud*.

> She wanted to drag up from some drowned region of human consciousness those very stones. She wanted to dive deep, deep, courageously down into some unexploited region of consciousness, into some common deep sea of unrecorded knowledge and bring, triumphant, to the surface some treasure buried, lost, forgotten. (P, p.179)

This speaks a yearning to plumb a realm of Otherness and to fish up its blood-purple 'murex'–the shell-yielding stain of a royal election.

Visiting the tombs by moonlight, travelling through allées of sphinxes, seeing the hieroglyphs stand forth, especially chick and giant bee, Helen knows the male/female couple is contained by a larger, more formidable and basic presence: the mother: 'As if they in some strange exact and precious period of pre-birth, twins, lovers, were held, sheltered beneath some throbbing heart' (P, p.220). The dome of the sky itself, pollenated with stars, the temple she hallucinates inside the temple they visit, all point to the maternal envelopment which H.D. made her character experience. She compares the limpid and gorgeous presence of light and stars ('flower dust') to living inside a flowering dome, a honeycomb, on the pregnant tip of flowering columns (ibid., p.211).

'Twin virile girls' (Helen and Mary) then explore by day the temple that Helen and Rafton had explored by night. Here the evanescent vision of the presence of Otherness is signalled by the recurrence of the blue flash of Isis, the major Egyptian goddess who is appealing as the thief from Ra of the secret name of the paternal god, as the questor for Osiris, and as the mender of a broken male body, so the cause of recurrent fertility, even after fragmentation and dismemberment. (So if James Joyce was right, surely T.S. Eliot was wrong – or incomplete. Something he later felt as well.) Now in both 'Hipparchia' and 'Murex' there is an Egyptian subtext; in both earlier sections, Isis is imported even a little awkwardly but with fervour to assist, as would be appropriate, at remembering, and at 'remembering differently' – trying to exit from patriarchal thought.[20] Isis herself as 'bird-blue goddess' appears to Hipparchia (P, p.83); Ermy, a Nefertiti-like 'Jewess' in blue faces Raymonde (ibid. p.126). And in that Jewishness, as in Bloom's, another cross-light of otherness is evoked.

53

But in the final section, the hero/ine, Helen, unknowingly enacts Isis as, in a stunning blue get-up, she enters that Egyptian temple in the moonlight and receives *Raf*ton's illuminating message (winning some occult knowledge from the patriarchs): that Greece came to Egypt to learn (ibid., p.215). This promptly, though obscurely, occurs. She retraces their route the next day with Mary, and, in a birth-like motion, swings herself through the exact space of the Niké temple she had, the night before, hallucinated (as if part of the Parthenon were superimposed on Karnak). Thus she is reborn – as 'Helios and Athene' might gloss this – as a fused symbol of creativity and procreativity. All this rebirth is articulated in a temple of Otherness, ripe with 'some mystic suggestion, subtle, over-riding, over-bearing the stark Olympians, suggestion, subtle that made one, illiterate, drop, drop down from the edge of the flat earth into some realm, deep, hidden from the curious, prodding brain' (ibid., p.230). This in Egypt, the country of otherness, which is described as 'another planet' (ibid., p.226). And this visionary authority is presided over by the female goddess Isis, manifesting herself, in Helen's day vision, as an intense blue colour. 'Iris blue, iris green, iris bright-blue, iris wet-blue, altogether different, a blue brighter than the brightest that can ever be named' (ibid., p.233). The metonymic exchange or connection of Isis for iris had been made completely explicit earlier: "Iris; I don't really think of iris here. It's so essentially a Greek flower. But *Isis*, it's almost the same thing" (ibid., p.226). The secret name, finally, is Isis, as of course it will be in *Helen in Egypt*.

Some of the unifying power of the Isis figure for H.D. can be surmised from this summary from *Pilate's Wife* (1924):

Isis was a magician and goddess of wisdom. The Greeks . . .

had had to split the perfect image of the perfect Woman, say here is Love, faithless, and here is Wisdom, loveless. Yet even Aphrodite and Athene, re-modelled, flung into some blasting furnace, to return one perfectly welded figure, would yet lack something – something of the magic that Isis held in Egypt.[21]

Sexual woman and wise woman, woman as mother and lover: Isis is the Other beyond dualism, an expression of H.D.'s desire for transcendent presence in *female* form.

When H.D. writes of maternal Otherness, it is manifested in language in a particular way: racing, dynamic, meditative and associative, in punning substitution (iris/Isis). *Palimpsest*, a central thematic sourcebook for later poems like *Trilogy* and *Helen in Egypt*, also marks a transition between the static, somewhat turgid, 'over-intense' voice and a freer, bolder, sometimes essayistic, relatively unmasked personal voice that is visible in *The Gift*, in *Tribute to Freud*, even in *HERmione*, and certainly in *Trilogy* (NRW, pp.9/10).

In an important reading to which this analysis is indebted, Deborah Kelly Kloepfer argues that H.D.'s task in these prose works of the mid to late 1920s could best be glossed by Julia Kristeva's work establishing a register of discourse before paternal sign and law. This anterior voice is pre-Oedipal. Kloepfer argues that H.D. successfully transmutes the problematic of the maternal (restrictions, repressions, rejections, hatreds even to matricidal fantasies) into access to the maternal which occurs in a special 'textual rhythm' (Kloepfer, 1984, p.32). The rhythms and repetitious pulsing prose, associated with the heritages of maternal and homosexual otherness, proposes not a polarity between (male) and speech and (female) silence but a new speech, the speech of the Other.

As 'one writing . . . erased to make room for another',

palimpsest is an idea with a good deal of resonance in H.D.'s mental life beyond the title of one book. It locates the interplay between rhythms of association and the search for basic truth which characterises the intellectual and aesthetic texture of her best work. The original writing would leave, on a parchment, shadow, on a wax tablet, grooves (a word H.D. uses in *Tribute to Freud*; cf. Freud's 'Mystical Writing Tablet') which the new writing might have a tendency to follow or at least to rediscover. These grooves or shadows may be sign of a basic reality or they may be simply suggestive signifying accidents. At all times in a palimpsest there is foreground and background, new statement and obscured original, an original which can be discovered with the force of a revelation or something left overwritten in undecidable layering. For H.D., the original idea behind the idea would have final dominance, but the mysterious random process of associative and accretive decoding is the only path to it.

Palimpsest may suggest the metonymic chain, a series of tellings of something with no one ever having final dominance, an evocation of plurality and multiplicity, lack of finality. This suggests the porousness of H.D.'s style, its unauthoritarian, constantly exploratory quality, despite this firm appeal to a final truth, saved from the embarrassments of authority precisely by being perpetually hidden as well as being exactly different from what dominant culture offers. The word palimpsest textualises mind, history, reality. To understand is to read, decode, translate, but there is always something not fully decipherable.

For H.D., film, as one critic has summarised, 'functions as a psychic medium externalizing and making perceptible invisible inward intentions and coherencies' (Morris, 1984, p.423). This description could as well characterise the third grouping of H.D.'s prose, which I have called the 'Borderline' group because it is very indebted to avant-garde cinema and its developing poetics as articulated by some of H.D.'s associates from the late 1920s through to about 1933–34.[22] These included Bryher, Kenneth Macpherson (to whom H.D. was introduced, astonishingly, by Frances Gregg), a man with whom she was fiercely in love, and whom Bryher married after her divorce (1927) from her first husband, Robert McAlmon (Guest, p.178 ff.). The three became, for a while, an intense ménage, Barbara Guest calls it, wonderfully, a 'menagerie of three', alluding to their pet names: Fido for Bryher, Rover for Macpherson (inclined that way), Cat for H.D., And for Perdita for whom they all cared, differently, with a firm and wayward love, their name was Pup (Guest, p.188). (H.D. chose to abort her Macpherson pregnancy in 1928).

The POOL cinema group with *Close Up*, the original journal concerning film as art, felt it could achieve in cinema the invisible Otherness at the core of things. That is, film was, for them, the medium of Otherness, linked intellectually and psychologically to psycho-analysis, and based not on mimetric realism but on mental processes, including fantasy, juxtaposition, desire, repression.[23] H.D. participated in Macpherson–Bryher's cinematic ventures: acted in several productions, contributed to *Close Up*, reviewed films, and in a number of ways drew on the milieu, and interpreted the meaning of this new form in her narratives and poems. Her critique of Hollywood cinema in 'The Cinema and the Classics' series joined her contempt for banal versions of romance with her desire to offer democratic access to a spiritual reality.[24] No need to naturalise or homogenise otherness: in film, through the unique qualities of the medium, the position and receptivity of the audience, the evocation of mystery (with fades and super-impositions) and the ability to suggest interior states by a lingering over exterior objects, otherness can exert its special powers.

Borderline (1930) is the name of the only surviving complete film in which H.D. acted and which she may have helped edit; it is also the title of a pamphlet she wrote about the film (Guest, p.197). As an idea or psychic stance, borderline seems to propose hypo-cathexis, or intense projection of self into a desired person, and narcissism, or a fraught peering into one's own hidden otherness. There are as well political, social and racial dimensions implied by the plot of the film, which expresses pressures and crises of liminality and identification in an oblique melodrama of cross-racial romance and jealousy. The word 'borderline' implies the porous vulnerable moment of crossing which scrambles differentiation of persons ('We're not three separate people. We're just one') but which might also induce so much identification and fusion with others that it could produce confusion and inauthenticity, a loss of self symbolised in 'Narthex' by much superficial chatter, put-downs and resistance to saying what is really felt.[25] This prose in general, upon which much more critical work needs to be done, strikes an overscrupulous note, although many notable H.D. motifs exist therein.

It is true, however, that H.D.'s interest in cinema and elements of her 'borderline' aesthetic – including a critique of dominant narrative, dependence on projec-tion, fixations on other dimensions of experience than the surface reality – are evident in all her novels after the POOl cinema group forms in 1927, no matter to which of the three groupings I have said they belong: so *Palimpsest*, as well as *HERmione*, not only *Kora and Ka et al.*

work with cinema in ways that need more elucidation. Certainly, like much modernist practice, the borderline aesthetic attempts a 'welding of the psychic or super-normal to the things of precise everyday existence' (H.D.'s pamphlet for *Borderline*, cited by Morris, 1984, p.425). In addition, deep psychic fluctuations – in all their compelling, compulsive repetitions – are foregrounded as tone, mood, character and action.

The lens H.D. uses in *HERmione* (or in later work like *Bid Me to Live*) catches herself oddly because she is, so to speak, both 'cinematographer' and main subject, behind the camera and in front of it, actor and *auteur*. She is then both the object of sight, caught as the awkward over-intense beauty, and the subject, since interior mono-logue is a main technique of these novels. H.D. writes a cinematographer's monologue, visual patterns, dis-solves, superimpositions and the cock-eyed vision of consciousness with its own distortions and angles are all rendered in the prose. Behind and in front of the 'camera', she examines herself, or the similacrum of herself in the mirror her prose creates. She analyses her own gestures in her own gaze. I have already mentioned the insistence on mirroring and palimpsest in style; sentence by sentence gaze is caught, refracted back, caught again: 'Behind the Botticelli, there was another Botticelli, behind London there was another London, behind Raymonde Ransome there was (odd and slightly crude but somehow "taking" nom-de-guerre Ray Bart' (P, p.104).

This may be narcissism, but it is also an experiment in attempting a kind of female subject not centred by what has been called the 'male' gaze of the lens. H.D.'s auto-biographical projections can escape dominant narrative and representation by what is surely near solipsistic in-trospection, but is also a way of controlling the gaze, so that she possesses her own look – and her own disjunctive split self: name and pseudonym – by mirrorings both thematic and stylistic, and possesses a tremendous historical and mythic space, by palimpsest. The singleness, solipsism and narcissism apparent on the surface are some results of experiments in ending the dichotomy of subject and object, of observer and observed.

'Madrigal cycle', another more major set of 1920s novels, all concern the emergence of a woman artist.[26] Madrigal refers, of course, to a capella part singing in close harmony, offering various distinctive voices tracing intricate melodic and contrapuntal relations. It should be clear that 'madrigal' can be construed as forming horizontally what 'palimpsest' does vertically – a set of layered materials which intersect, through which one must read the interplay of present and past. Madrigal, with its high and low, chiming and descanting voices, is also a tribute to the autobiography which provoked these works, H.D.'s lesbian and heterosexual intensities (her love for Frances Gregg and Ezra Pound), the weaving in of the same people time and again (like versions of Aldington), the echoes of similars (like Bryher and Gregg), the repetition of events (sexual desire, pregnancy, adultery, artistic and personal turmoil), and the recurrent thematics of romance, betrayal, loss, gender debate, alienation and ambition. H.D., seems to have made some strategic choices about the versions of this 'story' which she published, repressing the lesbian passions that framed this period from 1905–19 to concentrate on the socially and narratively palatable heterosexual plots.[27] For example, she left unpublished *Paint it To-day*, a Hawthorne-influenced, lesbian essay-novel based on her first trip to Europe (1911) with Frances Gregg. And she left unpublished the *Kunstlerroman HERmione* which frankly and lavishly presents a debate between conventional sexuality and lesbian choices, a quest to self as Other, as 'Her', chronicling the formation of a poet from a safe and sorry adolescent in nine generative months.[28]

The difficulty of establishing female identity as subject is signalled by H.D.'s cunning nickname for her main character, Hermione. That object case, used in subject place, exactly locates the thematics of the self-as-woman: 'surveyor and surveyed', who pointedly explores the selfhood she can make from articulating her Otherness.[29]

Not knowing what else to do with her sense of failure and her so far callow longings for life, exasperated by family ties, Hermione essays a conventional plot: she falls in love and wants to marry. She thereby attempts to reject her sense of difference, which is articulated through her friendship with Mandy, the family's black maid, her desire for a sister with whom she could 'run' and her wrenching ambivalence to her mother. 'It is better really to give in to people, be quite ordinary and quite happy like all people' (HER, p.224). Eugenia, once convinced of the at least semi-propriety of Hermione's engagement to the bohemian poet, George Lowndes (based on Pound), settles into the social advantage and surface pleasures of marrying off her daughter to a fine man and his even finer mother.

At the moment she finally pleases her mother, Her finds she must break the engagement because of an intensified involvement with her friend Fayne, which marks the second half of the novel. But Fayne, having almost wilfully disturbed normal courtship rituals by lesbian passion, suddenly reveals to Her that she has had a secret relationship with George. Since the choice between George and Fayne had increasingly appeared as a choice of identities (wife/muse *vs.* lesbian/poet), Her breaks down completely when she rejects one and is betrayed by the other. A number of the thematic motifs that Gilbert and Gubar summarise as part of the interplay between anxiety and authority occur here: images of enclosure and desire for escape; outrageous doubles (Fayne) of externally docile egos (Hermione); disease (the illness *cum* breakdown at the end); even the strange presence of the other in the house – *HERmione's* peculiar ending (Gilbert and Gubar, *Madwoman*, passim). But she is reborn, sure of being Her, the one who is Otherness. Her's accrued authority comes from the saturation in related sources of Otherness: maternal/sororal mirroring and access to a visionary level of language which the novel repeatedly traces.

There is the otherness of Mandy, who has a great appreciation, Her says, of 'the finer distinctions of the English language' (HER, p.27). They are mirrored as two sets of hands reach to and fro into a bowl of cherries to pit them: 'Her slipped a white hand into the deep bowl, black arm lifted from the deep bowl' (ibid.). Mandy's difference is shown as valuable to Her in and for itself; Mandy also prefigures and contains both other sources of the maternal and sororal mirrors.

There is the otherness of an articulated maternal connection. In the mid-book scene with her mother during which Eugenia recalls the circumstances of Her's birth, at which Mandy (lacking the doctor) had assisted as midwife, Her is swept into feeling. The passionate and fiery storm that unites the women as Eugenia speaks a funny, pulsing language re-articulated Her's moment of birth. Mandy (here called 'Demeter') 'was like a mother to me', said Her's own mother (ibid., p.89). The mother–daughter chain possesses a mystery; the father–daughter tie does not rival it: 'Eugenia is Eleusinian. My father is Athenian' (ibid., p.31). Images of a luminous globe of light and 'tidewave of tidal waters' mark the moment when Her finds a necessary answer to paternal and fraternal intellection, science, career. 'Words of Eugenia had more power than textbooks, than geometry (ibid., p.89). So in a parallel scene in *To the Lighthouse*, Lily Briscoe, her head on Mrs Ramsay's lap, knows that her feelings cannot be 'written in any language known to men'.[30] H.D. and Woolf posit thematically, and enact linguistically, a set of strategies which, in this situational context, one can call the language of otherness.

By the incantatory speech in which Eugenia returns Hermione to her own birth, Her gains access to a 'maternal, "semiotic" register' of language and feeling: cadenced pulsations of speech, identification and fusion in feeling, and repetitive, mirroring, associative language, rendering of the slow play of consciousness in, around and through daily life (having breakfast, making a phone call, walking a dog) (Kloepfer, 1983, p.28). But Eugenia's idea of writing ('those dear little stories you did', parallel, undoubtedly, to H.D.'s own dim beginnings: moralistic sub-Alcott feuilletons in Protestant magazines) makes Her blanch (HER, p.80). Hence Eugenia alone (without both Mandy and then Fayne) has 'no midwife power, you can't lift me out of this thing', thinks Her, of her depression (ibid.). Her needs both her black and her white mothers; she also needs her lesbian sister.

As in Dorothy Richardson's *Pilgrimage* in which Miriam's access to speech is mediated through a mirroring relationship of envelopment and lesbian desire, so here the passages of lesbian bonding are intensely described, and strongly related to the kind of writing Her desires. Fayne's hands stroke Her's throat, source of the voice, Her's hands stroke Fayne's head, one source of desire, or hands threaten to strangle, with playful malice; in this stroking secret messages are sent and received. Finally a kiss is exchanged which, as a moment of lesbian consummation, is comparable to – and even beyond – the power of George's sylvan chase which climaxes in a more grinding, dubious kiss.[31] By virtue of chronicling the attachment of Fayne and Her, the work makes a critique of heterosexuality as a social institution, bringing into the text some daring, important elements: woman-to-woman bonding, female erotic desire, and making a study, as well, of the pain and manipulativeness of lesbian, as of heterosexual, relationships.

Fayne creates an atmosphere of intensity and knowledge in which subject and object (she and her) twin and double each other, mirror each other, and reproduce themselves by doubled words. With Fayne, new kinds of words, 'projections of things beyond one' occur easily (HER, p.146). The image patterns entering the scenes with Fayne reveal interpenetration of identities, leading thematically to Hermione's self-identification as neither fanciful fiancée nor dutiful daughter, but as Her, a site in which language can be produced, and the 'white power' (of sexuality, visionary sensitivity, and identity) expressed (ibid., p.180).

The novel had begun in the absence of her effective speech, expressed by discontent over both her given and her family names and bafflement about the evocative tie between words and things. Hermione's attraction to George depends on his vocation as poet and his already existing mastery of the scripts and poses of a literary courtship. Yet she finds his desire for a 'decorative' muse cages her in a feminine self without acknowledging 'the thing back of the thing', a moral and aesthetic touchstone (ibid., pp.172, 198). Her has wanted George to rescue her, choose for her in choosing her; this feminine passivity is later punctured in a comic description of a painting of Perseus rescuing his maiden (ibid., p.134). For he is neither her romantic ideal, nor able to comprehend her ('George doesn't know what I am'), or even to keep up with her ('not attuned to high beating intellect that had raced ahead of him') (ibid., pp.84, 85). These notions also occur in the Undine analogy George proposes, of a mermaid who loses both voice and feet. He did not know or care about seismographs or amoebae, and he confused the exact names of flowers, in a book which mentions literally hundreds of varieties (ibid., pp.116–19).

Finally, he is not sufficient to focus her growing ambition as a writer, since he nastily retracts his crowning praise of her poems at his own romantic, jealous whim (ibid., pp.149, 167). With George, words are judgements passed (ibid., p.133). Affected by George, she is compared to a child with a primer, to a barely articulate foreigner (ibid., p.93). This is because George, like the male writers in *Bid Me to Live*, has an ambivalent appreciation of her ambition as a poet. He cites an emblematic line from Browning that curtails her in the objectified role of inspiration, muse, matrix for his creative urge: 'You are a poem though your poem's naught' (ibid., p.212).

Fayne, in contrast, has a more positive effect on Her's ability to speak. Talking to Fayne is mannered but deep; Fayne's hands on her throat electrify the site of speech (ibid., p.145). Fayne also has an allusive but intense interest in her poetry, signalled by the singing swallow, loyal to memory and desire, of Swinburne's 'Itylus', which is cited repeatedly. With Fayne, words are projections and luminosities, terms evoking new arts like cinema and a poetic practice based on visualisation.

H.D. argues that the accomplished, even notorious avant-garde poet, based on Pound, is excelled and surpassed by these two provincial girls who can touch their roots in otherness.

And these roots are bared in amazing passages of mirroring and identification. Her seems to give birth to Fayne: 'She is some amplification of myself like amoeba giving birth, by breaking off, to amoeba. I am a sort of mother, a sort of sister to Her' (ibid., p.158). This non-sexual reproduction is a serio-comic identification with some lowly 'others' of the protozoan kingdom, which, like women, perhaps, 'characteristically have an indefinite, changeable form' (a dictionary says). When they kiss, 'Her bent forward, face bent toward Her': a mirroring moment in the syntax (ibid., p.163). And in both of these passages, the careful, colourful capitalisation of the word 'her' points to the fusions and discoveries of the self, the healing of splits and fragments which Her feels in her passion, while it is not clear if Her gives birth to her (Fayne) or to Her (herself), because H.D. clearly means to indicate both. This intricate play with names, pronouns, selves, identities and the powers of otherness comes to a climax when Her strokes Fayne's head: 'I will not have her hurt. I will not have Her hurt. She is Her. I am Her. Her is Fayne. Fayne is Her. I will not let them hurt HER' (ibid., p.181). Even the (possibly American dialect) repetition of sounds in 'hurt' and 'her' is declarative.

The racing mind and passionate desire of late Victorian Hermione, then, prophesy some of the major artistic and cultural breakthroughs of the modernist era: cinema, non-representational art, psychoanalysis and textual feminism. There are freeze frames, strange camera angles, intense close-ups of objects, fades, interesting montages or super impositions of eyes, of pools, of concentric circles – describing Fayne and Her, H.D. makes Her's mind work cinematically. In Her's visualisations occur wonderful avatars of such modern styles as constructivism, cubism, surrealism, impressionism and abstract painting (ibid., pp.6, 73, 60, 23, 52). H.D. also hints at explanations from psychoanalytic theory of her characters' 'difference'. Further, H.D. takes and reformulates the mannered pastoral/troubadour poems by Pound to her which cast her as Lady, muse, icon, object. Rupturing these icon-poems along the length and breadth of the novel, H.D. thereby makes a feminist revision of textual frames for woman (Friedman, *Poesis*, forthcoming). And she enhances textual feminist explorations by her prosodies of otherness in the textures of prose.

If the proof of this future artist lies in her native or intuitive experimental capacities for possession of the major movements and critiques of the modern era, the novel is also cunning in its subtext proving to the family that Hermione did not 'fail' any of the 'subjects' which gave her so much trouble as a freshman; indeed, her method of succeeding was more nuanced and complete, H.D.'s revisionary answer to the encoded demands of the paternal line. Botany and maths are endless sources for image and metaphor. She shows how well she knows both; indeed, she will 'prove them wrong' by words which 'supersede a scheme of mathematical–biological definition' by the 'mythopeic mind (mine)' (HER, p.76).

This proud polemical notion of Her's intuitive access to a critical modernism is paralleled in the earlier *Paint it To-day* by the hero/ine's accession to analytic and perceptive power by identification with and love for women. Acknowledging her passion for Josepha, Midget 'surprised [a curious] secret or found the door to another world, another state of emotional life or being . . .' (PIT,

Ch.I, pp.15–16). It is an 'emotional white truth' (ibid., Ch.III, p.2) that unifies but surpasses all the colour of the rainbow: the colour of lesbian Otherness is the colour of unity and light. As paradigm-breaking as Paul's conversion at Tarsus, acknowledged lesbian passion becomes a standard against which other claims to love's intensity can be tested. As well, the strong commitment to marginalisation, which lesbianism involves, gives a vantage from which other experiences of otherness can be tested. The early chapter that declares Midget's love for Josepha is followed by a chapter-essay on marginality and foreignness. Tourism (the young women are making the Grand Tour with Josepha's mother) offers them a peculiar sense of election as Americans to sensuality, intensity and epiphany – experiences that the whimsical, sophisticated Europeans are said to miss. Here too H.D. insists that proto-expatriation and marginalisation from both social and sexual covenants lead these young ladies to know much, more even than élites or artists.

Racial difference, maternal mirroring and lesbian sororal passion are related – and positive – forms of Otherness in this novel. All are involved with a frame-breaking, time-leaping, visionary perception (as seeing Mandy as an Etruscan bronze), and with crossings of borders, as between night and day (HER, p.88). Capacity for visionary sight, lesbian love, and matrisexuality all are summed up in a final image of powerful identity:

> Her was held like a star invisible in daylight that suddenly by some swift adjustment of phosphorescent values comes quite clear. Her saw Her as a star shining white against winter daylight. (ibid., p.225)

She is the 'lady . . . set back in the sky', she a new anti-patriarchal constellation (ibid., p.76).

Boundarilessness and identification with women are in all ways treated positively in this novel, despite the plot of betrayal. Indeed, making lesbianism a coequal possibility in the romance plot is a radical act. An 'anti-Oedipal' plot, the question of individuation/separation has been broached not only in the series of anti-romance decisions at the end of the novel (the significant use of her trousseau money not to marry but to travel to Europe), but in the prose throughout. Fluidity, overlapping identifications and fusions as in the remarkable passages that concern Fayne, assertions that 'people are in things, things in people' instate boundarilessness in a positive fashion as the mode of discourse throughout (ibid., p.198).

In a study of female narrative, Nancy Miller calls attention to the explicitly phallocentric model for plots (thus for the shape of female desires) which has made the ambition and quest in women's plots unreadable. The 'repressed content [of these plots] would be not erotic impulses, but an impulse to power; a fantasy of power that would revise the social grammar in which women are never defined as subjects: a fantasy of power that disdains a sexual exchange in which women can participate only as objects of circulation' (Miller, in Showalter (ed.), p.348). Readers of *Hedylus*, *Palimpsest*, *HERmione* can credit the varieties of female desire which H.D., with growing boldness, explores: matrisexual, lesbian, female-identified, which become both fuel to and fire of that impulse to power which reverses the object status of woman in an assumption of the powers of Otherness: maternal, sororal, visionary. 'Star sprinkling from a wild river.'

Chapter Three

Gender Authority: 'Another Region of Cause and Effect, Another Region of Question and Answer'

> She is a woman,
> yet beyond woman,
> yet in woman . . . [1]

Advent, a revised journal H.D. kept as an analysand of Sigmund Freud, indeed announces something momentous: the beginning of a cluster of works that have a magisterial status in her *oeuvre*, both major autobiographical exploration and major revisionary myths in which '. . . the ghost itself of all our lives comes visually before us'.[2] H.D. went to Freud in Vienna at the end of the interwar period, at a time when Nazism was beginning to assert terroristic and totalitarian force, at the time of its seizing of state power in Germany (February–March 1933), and its attempted *putsch* in Austria (July 1934). She had about twenty weeks of analysis in 1933 and 1934 during a dangerous political crisis whose impact she registered. She went simultaneously as student/colleague (potential lay analyst) and as patient to examine her blocked or compromised achievement.[3]

H.D.'s discontent with her writing for the ten years from about 1925–35 was not writer's block, since, as we have seen, her literary production was continuous, but it involved a fear of repetition, a discomfort both with what she dubbed her 'hallucinated writing' (possibly the Borderline or *Magna Graeca* prose) and with the 'Air and Crystal' of the imagist period (ETT, p.35). Her writing, she said, 'had reached a vanishing point of sterility and finesse'; it is 'all on that high-vibration-to-the-breaking-point level'.[4] Even about *Palimpsest*, H.D. could later say that 'the writing is weedy and involved, with many baffling parentheses' (NRW, p.69).

In the diagnostic title poem for an unpublished collection, *A Dead Priestess Speaks*, H.D. further reveals a condition of feminine over-compliance. 'Circumspect', a word that recurs, the poet feels she had been too 'good', 'quiet and still by day', a risklessness keeping repressed her passionate opinions (CP, pp. 370, 372, 373, 376; 377, 369). Contributing to her discontent was the peculiar status of those prose works from the 1920s which have a lesbian component. Because H.D. did not brook the powerful social taboo, such works as *Asphodel, Paint it Today, and HERmione* – works in which she had made a large investment of emotional energy, craft and time – were left unpublished. If style separates autonomously as she diagnoses about some of her novels, if poem does not apparently lead to oeuvre, as in the whole abandoned collection *A Dead Priestess Speaks*, if composition splits from publication as in the 'Madrigal cycle', a writer might justifiably feel dissociated, fragmented, incomplete.

This discontent had broader political sources, as did its analysis and cure. H.D. felt her self had been undermined and devastated politically and personally by World War I, by the historical and psychic disintegration therein represented, whose depiction and analysis form a significant theme in H.D.'s work: militarism is decried, and the anti-generative and anti-erotic world view, the eradication of spiritual knowledge, and masculinist mentalities are probed repeatedly.[5]

A series of formative tragedies between 1915 and 1919 (as central to H.D. as the terrible chain of family deaths of 1895–1906 were for Woolf) had marked H.D. in her early efflorescence. In 1915, there was a stillborn baby about which she tersely reports in *Asphodel* 'Khaki killed it'.[6] The drowning of civilians in the sinking of the *Lusitania* signalled a profound change in the conduct of wars: women and children and other noncombatants were as vulnerable to fire-power and semi-legitimate violence as any soldier. A good deal of H.D.'s work occurs to register, absorb and transform this political reality. Her brother Gilbert was killed in action (1918), and her father, precipitously dead in response to that loss (1919). Metaphorically, she lost a husband, for Richard Aldington and she were permanently estranged, in part because he identified strongly with militaristic manhood. They separated once in 1918, definitively in 1919, divorced in 1938. She lost two male friends, D.H. Lawrence, a 'twin brother' with whom she had strong bonds in 1916–18, and Cecil Gray, the father of Perdita. And she almost lost that baby and herself as well, for she was near death-stricken with the influenza (and/or pneumonia) in 1919, just before her daughter's birth in March. This complex of personal events, themselves deeply marked by the war, fused in what she named her 'war-phobia', the transcendence of which became a major psychological and literary project for more than twenty years, in part accomplished by her noncombatant's trial by fire in the London Blitz of World War II.

So it would be hard to overemphasise the roles of the two World Wars in H.D.'s imaginative and moral life. Indeed, the relation between them was like that between the Old and New Testaments: the one set problems and made prophecies which were only understood and redeemed in the second. The shock of World War II, which closed this 'Freud period', 'dynamited' long-repressed memories, in part by fear of 'complete physical annihilation'.[7] The fires, the bombing raids, the constant alarms of the Blitz, 'brought things to a burning focus and reality'.[8] War was the fire, and her life became the lens she held to that fearsome sun.

The not surprising prevalence of fire images had, as well, a special meaning. In H.D.'s view, fire was to break the 'crystalline' shell of her elegant and artful writing. For in a perceptive self-assessment, H.D. stated that she had perfected this 'crystalline' element but lacked fire in her writing, although the crystal indicated an impacted energy which promised a fire as yet unfulfilled. The interplay between fire and crystal is a subplot of *Notes on Recent Writing*. 'I grew tired to [sic] hearing these [early] poems referred to, as crystalline. Was there no other way of criticizing, of assessing them? But perhaps I did not see, did not dare see any further than my critics. Perhaps my annoyance with them was annoyance with myself' (NRW, pp.9/10).

But in the war, because of the war, 'the actual fire has raged round the crystal' (ibid., p.15). An intensity of visualisation, of memory, of nurturant autobiography in *The Gift* and then in *Tribute to Freud*, interleaved with the writing of *Trilogy*. This poem was 'runic, divinatory. This is not the "crystalline" poetry that my early critics would insist on. It is not pillar of salt nor yet of hewn rock-crystal. It is the pillar of fire by night, the pillar of cloud by day' (ibid., p.26). To achieve this fire three sources are tapped: the authority of her Otherness, as in novels of the 1920s; the critical and analytic authority she achieved in relation to Freud – the claim of intellectual coherence and emotional necessity for female gender authority; political/historical experiences which directly struggled with war phobia and fear of fire, a female bravery also based on her assumption of gender authority.

For Freud she saw as a rare kind of flame; with his 'radium-burning' he pierced 'that sort of crystal surface in me'.[9] With Freud, against Freud, through Freud she struggled for gender authority, for nuanced interpretations of her existence and experiences. H.D.'s analysis with Freud was a critical engagement with male discourse about men and women, and with the symbolic meanings of gender in Western religion and myth. This is Susan Friedman's point in *Psyche Reborn*; H.D.'s gender authority involves critical assimilation without acquiescence.[10]. The constant pattern of this engagement involved H.D.'s fascination by the explanatory force of Freud's ideas (e.g. about the pre-Oedipal, or the 'mother-fix', about bisexuality) but her refusal and subtle repudiation of his negative value judgements. The same pattern holds in H.D.'s revision of misogynistic myth: a critical 'interaction with tradition' by scrutiny of the 'androcentric roots of negative definitions' of women is followed by a 'subversive transformation' (Friedman, *Psyche Reborn*, p. 271). Both Freud, and the rationalist tradition, and myth as a spiritual tradition offered powerful sources of inspiration to which H.D. posed herself in powerful antithesis (ibid., p.231).

Further, as Friedman has repeatedly argued, H.D. associated twentieth-century historical disasters with gender polarisation and with the repression of the 'feminine' position, linked to her interest in the irrational and in female Otherness. Thus her reconstruction of self, and self-in-culture, led necessarily to an examination of gender. She formulated a critique of male gender authority in nurtured antagonism to the male mentor, here as elsewhere both inspired by – and inspired by resistant to – Freud.

In an apparently simple encounter with Freud's dog at her first appointment, the domesticity of the incident veiling and complicating the principle, H.D. says: 'The Professor was not always right.' She credits her 'intuition' which 'challenges' his judgement–but 'wordlessly'. Still she sees both his very male root and her very female tendril as part of the same 'common Tree of Knowledge' (TF, pp.98–9). Her challenge – more than a footnote or corrective to his mastery – suggests the presence of 'another region of cause and effect, another region of question and answer'. This 'region' she explores in her writing of this period.

In this intense listening to the strange statements of her visions, her intuitions, her *sotto voce* and *sub rosa*, even wordless, insights, H.D. offers her most profound tribute to Freud. For, as Hayden White reminds us,

> Freud's major contribution to the study of mental illness was the 'willingness to listen' and thus to reconstruct their neurosis or madness phenomenologically, from within their experience, reading/decoding their sign system. Thus Freud's main contribution was not the 'mechanistic formalism' of his systematic theory but the therapeutic technique, with its artistic and hermeneutic subtlety.[11]

In a passage full of Biblical allusions of the most flattering variety, H.D. first assimilates Freud by imagining herself 'salting my savourless writing' with Freud's actual utterances, as amenuensis, not writer (TF, p.148). Leaving her feminine, but phallic vial of smelling salts on his couch, thus revealing and releasing her 'penis envy', announces the terms of transference to the 'father', and apparently accepts Freud's idea that creative women are as nothing 'unless they had a male counterpart or a male companion from whom they drew their inspiration'. (ibid., p.149). She obligingly remembers Aldington and D.H. Lawrence, mingling them with Freud and Christ. The powerful, even adoring transference, which is directly presented in *Advent*, has, however, a subtext, cunningly and silently laid down, which allows its author into 'another region'.[12]

For the very night when she records her apparent approval of this law of the male muse, she dreams of her mother's velvet-framed, flower-painted mirror and says: 'I want a fusion or transfusion of my mother's art' (ibid., p.151). The muse for the woman artist is abruptly, critically extended. If 'transference' occurs between a women and a powerful male figure, still 'transfusion' occurs between one woman and another. So Freud as a paternal/maternal compound (the way he will be depicted in *Helen in Egypt*) focused H.D. on her double demand: transference and transfusion, simultaneous – not sequential – pre-Oedipal and Oedipal articulations. And works such as *Trilogy* show the emergence, in the post-Freud writing, of massive female symbols, resolutions and myths, of women-identified quests, and of female heroes who act in narratives making explicit critique of phallocentric culture. Transfusion has occurred, enabled and allowed by the impact of the analytic situation, but also by the gender powers H.D. already brought to it, and had enhanced in it.

The Gift, an autobiographical memoir about her family

history and Moravian origins, is a lucid, finished work, based, like *Tribute to Freud*, on apparently casual surfaces of free association among semi-related, semi-detached memories.[13] The writing of *The Gift* is deeply involved with the entrance into, and defence of other 'regions' which the Freud encounter enabled and the war triggered. It is her gift to herself, as *Tribute* was her gift to Freud.

Written with the nightly bombings of the Battle of Britain reverberating, written with fierce and moving meditations on the civilian experience of total war, this work must have seemed at all moments to be potentially H.D.'s last work, possibly even a lost work (lost to fires and rubble), yet her tapping typewriter provided her brave answer to the booming mortar shells. *The Gift* engages in a critical spiritual politics, where not only acts of imagination, but the dimensions, regions and materials to which these acts give access, respond to political terror with a domain of meta-knowledge.

Burning is the most ambiguous and potent recurrent image; from the stunning opening recalling a young girl, caught aflame in her own crinolines, burning to death at her grandfather's seminary, burning is often (though not always) associated with the vulnerability and preciousness of girls as symbols of life and sacrifices to it. The dead sister and half-sister, the dead first wife, evoke wonder and threat. The Bethlehem steelmills' fires make the trees (recall Dryad) vulnerable. Mamalie's whispered vision exposing the child to a rich mystical heritage is illuminated by a shadowy small candle floating in water. The child's monumental fear that a shooting star will fall on their family in fact predicts the terrors of war that occasioned this work. Fire tempers, tests, illuminates; it consumes, tortures, destroys. This work is, then, fire to fight fire: female fire, poet's fire, fires of outcasts, fires of vision to counter Blitz fires and the explosions of war.

The various fires, more than linking sections dia-chronically (historically) signal the meshing of layers of memory to call back recurrent central questions – of gift, of salvation, of vision. Like any work in the medium of language, *The Gift* unrolls in narrative and syntactic time. But H.D.'s intent, studied, important use of allusions binding chapter to chapter – allusions to fires, to clocks, to snakes/alligators, to wars, to Christmas rituals, to an inspiriting wind – suggests that the book is, arguably, not linear but layered, palimpsested. From 'Morning Star', the final annunciatory section and the only one completely in present time, we can look 'down' and back into the pool of individual time, and find memories and manifestations which have historical concentricities as do circles made in water and are meant to be synchronous (simultaneous) presences.

The domestic events of *The Gift* are never domesti-cated; mystery is never reduced but enhanced as the nexus of materials for new regions of cause and effect, new realms of explanation. *The Gift* not only gains a 'transfusion' from a maternal heritage of artistic and spiritual vision, but seems first, in a stunned encounter with her wounded father, and second, in an unspoken stammering revelation of some sexual abuse (by an anonymous teamster), thereupon to present the induce-ment to replacing transference with a heavy investment in 'transfusion'.[14]

The narration of the father's accident, the mysterious event of his wounding, however biographically con-tained, is made psychologically fearsome.[15] The knowl-edge of male vulnerability articulated here in a mysterious wound, a concussion to the male head is a cunning reply to, or consideration of, the female body apparently wounded by so-called castration, but also by sexual abuse (that is by the knowledge of gender power-relations). So little Hilda's frightened jump from the teamster's cart, always repressed, and occurring obliquely in her sense that she was, perhaps, no longer a virgin (G, pp.50-9), is implicitly compared to her father's more public agony in his absent-minded fall from a moving trolley. Placed in the narrative just after the gift of second sight and Pentacostal vision descends through the maternal line, her father's brain and consciousness, and other male pressures are rejected now that young Hilda has found an alternative source which has the potential to answer powerlessness from the muted maternal side, through mystical intuition, not scientific positivism or proto-phallic probings.

The music of Mamalie, who closed her spinet permanently after experiencing Pentacostal possession and speaking in tongues, and the music of Mama, who never sang again after her father disparaged her voice, are both pressure and inducement to Hilda to complete the unfinished artistic and visionary work of her two mothers, work which had been compromised by personal fear and paternal judgement. For 'the gift' of second sight with which the book is concerned is a unity of a way of knowing and the insights gained which could be summed up in the word 'vision', and is the summation itself of a number of stances and strategies for female authority.

For claiming gender authority necessarily occurs by several, even contradictory strategies. First, there is the necessity to displace or replace the brother, but offer herself as a further-seeing gift to the father. This kind of ploy, infinitely laden with guilt and fear, is visible in the response of H.D. to the death (1934) of a fellow analysand, the flyer and intellectual Van de Leew, and may be part of her 'war phobia' after the death of Gilbert in 1918. In part the strategy of replacement asks the father (Freud in the first example) to be satisfied with her self, her possibility, her vision.

Yet, in narrative after narrative patterns, H.D. treats ambiguously whether she presents him with the needy female self, the daughter, as the moving, transcendent, even sentimentalised end of *Tribute to Freud* ('Writing on the Wall') tells, with its paternal 'Guardian' and 'Protector' of the baby soul. Or, in another strategy, whether she presents him with the 'Princess' who 'must find the baby' Moses, thus posing herself as the maternal protector of Freud (TF, pp.36-7). And not only the protector, but 'leaping over every sort of intellectual impediment and obstacle' (again the activity of vision), as the mechanism of Freud's immortality, the way that 'the Professor would be born again' (ibid., p.39). By one token, H.D. may be asking whether female presence could ever be sufficient, a question easily assimilated to theories of female lack. By another token, the whole muted mythic history of 'the race' is a region or a system that, composed psychologically ('the childhood of the individual is the childhood of the race' [ibid., p.38]), answers that theory. And the answer? Despite Freudian (and Lacanian) postulates: there is no lack in women: there is difference but not lack. And further, the gender authority of woman is primary. It exists, it has always existed, and H.D.'s 'business' is simply to prove this region of question and answer. As she said in 1949, the Freud analysis assisted her in reasserting 'my faith in an almost vanished mother-symbol' (NRW, p.47).

'She is a woman,/ yet beyond woman/ yet in woman' could surely point to this kind of authority: of the womb (to return to *Notes on Thought on Vision*) which is 'in woman' yet also 'beyond' her, as anyone with a failed pregnancy – stillbirth, miscarriage – could testify. That is, the power to give birth is a consummate gender power having intellectual and religious import. The impact of this female power is recorded in the race's primary and original icons, but that power is not always successful. Which H.D. knew.

At the same time, this gender authority and the vision that comes with it is positioned in a culture that not only denies its import and meaning, but insists that, for any authority, a female can never suffice, and the female must claim, metaphorically, 'really' or however, a phallic state or condition to be believed. This is the gist of a reading by Claire Buck, beginning from the Lacanian position that language is 'founded on "the feminine as its negative term"... and in order to speak the subject has to take up a position which is already sexed'.[16] For a woman poet, the speaking subject is problematised, because she cannot speak as a woman, but must speak as something else: Buck thus reads 'She is a woman/ yet beyond woman' to allude to the problem of the female speaking subject: that contradiction in terms also visible in 'Helios and Athene', not only suggests that phallic woman as one of H.D.'s several contradictorily interlocking solutions to claiming gender authority. These lines also suggest that the attempt to represent female gender authority by our conventions of representation has to proceed according to familiar metaphors and images. In this passage maleness is the way – for the purposes of an argument with Freud, as the poem is contextual – H.D. chooses to present the ecstasy and perfection of woman, precisely because it is the way she imagines Freud would be able to comprehend it. It may be that she appropriates maleness necessarily in order to speak at all, given her theoretical 'position in language'. But the use is over-determined: she may use these metaphors to speak to Freud, because he could understand female authority only by these terms.

Mamalie's matrilinear challenge to entranced Hilda–'to do the work' and to 'follow the music', permission to assume the authority of her gender in vision, in art, in politics–was to involve H.D. in a critique of authority, a critique of scepticism, and an emotional commitment to hidden or hermetic materials (G, p.89). This authority has a socio-political aspect, but it is the politics of vision. A 'Hidden Church' of tolerance, linked to mystical European heretical movements discussed in Denis de Rougemont's work, 'properly directed, might have changed the course of history...', in part by unifying any warring peoples (here Moravian and Shawnee) by the interlocking of their inner sanctum mysteries.[17] A universal heritage and spiritual language are H.D.'s goals: 'all nations and races met in the universal world of the dream' (TF, p.71).

So, going beyond *HERmione*, in *The Gift* the recovery of the maternal presence suggests a female spiritual politics: the female work of autobiography, based on fusion, not individuation, is matched by a female work in history, of empathetic identification and tolerance.[18] This is probably the 'grave philosophy' which H.D. felt she shared with Freud, the use of individual unconscious materials as mediations: individual quest to historical quest, particular or personal images and narratives as figures of myth, ancient story, and universal pattern (Friedman, *Psyche Reborn*, pp.73, 80, 83).

In this context it is again important to recall H.D.'s several uncanny and baffling visionary experiences, what she calls her 'writing on the wall'. Part of the gender authority she developed in her psychoanalysis lay in her refusal to compromise their force and impact, to accede to Freud's reduction of them to a 'dangerous symptom' of 'megalomania' (TF, p.51). As Friedman makes clear, Freud saw her visions as symptoms of a break with reality; H.D. saw them as signs of (and from) another reality (Friedman, *Psyche Reborn*, pp.100–1). She reclaimed various non-secular spaces of prophecy, of vision, and thus, in a *sub rosa* critique of Freud, she included a long exposition of the Corfu vision in *Tribute to Freud* despite occult experiences being 'outside the province of established psychoanalysis' (TF, p.39). The double valence of 'tribute'–as homage paid to a superior, and as exchange of gifts among equal royalty – seems nowhere more pertinent.[19]

In short, the emotional space created by H.D.'s two connections to Freud – transference to a father, and transfusion with a mother – allows a serious critical use of Freudian materials to mature in her major work. Working together at decoding still they saw 'things from different corners or sides of a room' (TF, p.119). Their sessions, as Susan Friedman has fully demonstrated,

> represent a prototypical confrontation between the polarities that permeate the modern world: man against woman, science versus religion, fact versus faith, objective versus subjective reality, reason versus intuition, the rational versus the irrational. (Friedman, *Psyche Reborn*, p.13)

H.D.'s attempt, in her claim to gender authority, is to rupture the universalising of male experience in Freud, to undermine or deflect the postulate, which reiterated a major element in Western philosophic and psychological tradition: that woman was deficient (ibid., p.122). For instance, Freud's idea that the original bisexuality of each individual never entirely disappears proved liberating to H.D. despite Freud's evaluation of all psychic or sexual manifestations of bisexuality as abnormal (ibid., pp.128–9). To be the 'perfect bi—', oscillating between sensual and erotic attractions to both sexes, defining oneself as doubled, meant that she was 'woman/ yet beyond woman,/ yet in woman' again as her poem about gender authority affirmed.[20] Again, the 'double demand' – for equality and difference both – is manifested. H.D. would be equal, and one of her metaphors for this is the phallic woman, with the 'dart and pulse of the male' (CP, p.456). She would be different; her main concern is to recover the 'almost vanished mother-symbol' (NRW, p.47).

The early revisionary impulse in H.D. thus came to majority by the assumption of gender authority in her debate with Freud: The studies like 'Eurydice' or the cross-temporal collaborations with Sappho, the historical re-animations of Hedylus and Hipparchia are like sketches, cartoons for the enormous and ambitious frescoes of the later period: the addition to the Bible in *Trilogy*; the rewriting of the Trojan War and epic in *Helen in Egypt*; the addition of a character to Shakespeare in *By Avon River*; the critique of American colonial violence and a patriotic myth in *The Gift*; the critique of theory, but not technique, in *Tribute to Freud*.

The composition of *Advent* (1933, and then 1948, both opening and closing this period of work) made her reflect, as for the first time, on a kind of rhythmic writing, although she seems to have originated it several years before in the 'pre-Oedipal' moments of *HERmione* and *Palimpsest*. This writing she interestingly characterises as 'only for cats and children'. By this shrug of one kind of verbal authority, she gains another: the kind of associative babble mixing high and low, lyric and exposition, sound and murmur almost without meaning which Kristeva postulates gives access to the 'chora' – an imagined primal space of plenitude based on the body of the archaic mother (TF, p.124).[21] This kid–cat writing becomes her mature style for both poetry and prose memoir. And it explains the aesthetic importance of the original journal, *Advent*, which led to both the Freud memoir and *The Gift*.

Freud's analytic procedure – the talking cure, the chains of free association, the metonymic combinations playing across the axis of selection to construct a swelling, interminable reading of any sign, this associative, ruminative, atemporal and palimpsested style – was already H.D.'s technical procedure (in *HERmione*) but until Freud she could not recognise that her palimpsested style, the voice of 'chora', was the definitive rupture from 'vanishing points of sterility and finesse'.

The foregrounding of this voice made H.D., like Woolf, a master of the essay. For the analytic power of a gender voice which chats to cats and children is extended in the generic choice of autobiographical essay memoir (*The Gift, Tribute to Freud,* then *End to Torment*) and in the epistemological stance of the essay as the form of a critique. Theodor Adorno's study 'The Essay as Form' pinpoints the way essays break several culturally normative dichotomies – of scientific understanding versus art, of objective/rationalist truth and subjective/mediated concepts. As well, Adorno posits that the essay form 'suspends the traditional [Cartesian] concept of method' and is a protest against Cartesian rules of thought. Instead of breaking the object of scrutiny into small analytic parts, the essay consistently dissolves the object back into its larger, fused contexts – ultimately the material and social interlock of life itself. Instead of beginning with the simplest and moving to the most complex, the essay begins with the complex and remains there because it wants to fuse materials in a force-field of interconnected elements. Instead of positing an exhaustive academic study, the essay thinks in fragments and foregrounds fissures, conflicts, discontinuities. It does not necessarily bring material to a unity but rather considers the fallible, provisional, and possibly personal nature of thought. Hence the essay is a critique of positivism: in its enthusiasms, its subjectivity, its open constructions, its scepticism of 'thought advancing in a single direction' is a deliberate creation of a formal and epistemological position which has the strongest analogies with one gender ideology: of female critique.[22] For all these reasons, the extended essay-memoir is the visible generic sign of the assumption of gender authority in H.D.

In *Trilogy*, as later in *Helen*, and in the 'medieval' romance of 'Hermetic Definition', H.D. poses some building-block stories of Western civilisation: the Trojan War, the Christian belief system, the quest narrative and its end in social regeneration and individual integration. By reinterpreting the women in these stories, she calls the authority of each tale into question. Her assumption of gender authority in the rescripting of these tales opens the narratives first by showing what they said in their deepest crevasses about women's psyche and social place, then by inventing a female perspective always implied, but never articulated, and finally by, as Robert Duncan has indicated, offering 'female revelation'.[23]

Trilogy was provoked by the intense social and spiritual vulnerability which H.D. experienced in London during the war years and especially in the Blitz. She felt, out of this terror, resurrected. In the three poems she traces, in a point-for-point argument, with a limpid structure made of triplings of all sorts, the means and meanings of that sense of rebirth from war, which was filled with apocalyptic images and structures of feeling.[24] Part of that newness was an intense prophetic or revisionary reading of myth: in these sites of spiritual renewal familiar female figures (Mary Magdalene, Mary Madonna, Venus, an unnamed but palpable Miriam) were reassessed in ways that altered traditional depictions.

Trilogy also engaged in a subtle interplay with Freudian materials, for in many ways it (along with *Helen in Egypt*) is the poem that redeems H.D.'s visionary experiences. For in it certain pictographs, analogous to the Corfu 'writing on the wall', organise the poem structurally. What was always at stake was how these mental materials were to be defined. Given the fact that Freud viewed her visionary states as 'dangerous', how could she prove that the hallucinations were more than benign but actively beneficient? She could, with an implicit critique of Freud's diagnosis, use these visions in her poetry, both directly, as narrative events, and indirectly as structural codes.

The tripod of the Delphic priestess which appeared directly in the projections of the Corfu vision is especially important to *Trilogy*.[25] It suggests H.D.'s desire to unite, in a post-Freudian synthesis, the three modes of thought or scientia to which Freud had so definitively contributed – religion, art and medicine. These three arts are seen, in *Tribute to Freud*, as unified in ancient times; now they can be reunited as 'a new form of thinking or of living' (TF, p.50); and, via H.D., as 'a new vehicle of expression'.

In 'The Walls Do Not Fall' there is, largely, an account of the gods/the goods whose 'shrines' have been metaphorically exposed under the bombing: 'ruin opens/ the tomb, the temple'; as it was in the archaeological digs at Karnak, so it is in the 'sliced walls' of London (CP, pp.509,510). This 're-valuing' of the gods/goods (a triple pun on which H.D. also plays in *Tribute to Freud* involving spiritual gods, emotional–ethical goods, material possessions) proffers a rich syncretic range variously organised (CP, p.538).

Now a major 'good' is the poet: in part this section is a defence of art – those walls which never completely fall – as the second poem defends religious vision and the third, the recurrent necessity for healing. H.D. makes a strong argument against the 'uselessness' of poets, a continuation of the debate with someone (Aldington, most likely) who, returning to a shell-shattered room after World War I 'gave a decisive football kick with his army boot to the fattest volume. . ... He demanded dramatically, "What is the use of all this–now?" (CP, p.517).[26] The opening section of *Trilogy* continues that argument between spiritual and–at least with that kind of boot and that kind of kick, masculinist–nihilist/ materialist positions. First, the experience of such an 'unstable' world where buildings sag and doors do not hang true on their lintels, where *'even the air / is independable'* leads to a strong quest motif; the blasting open of objects is equivalent to the blasting of paradigms on which our world was thought to be built (CP, p.543). In the aftermath of search, deeper and more satisfying sources of stability are revealed at the roots: the symbolic meaning of objects 'whose relative sigil has not changed/ since Nineveh and Babel' (ibid., p.523). Second, those who think 'what words say' and even more 'what words conceal' are '"pathetic"' and '"non-utilitarian"' receive a proud condemnation from H.D. (CP, p.517). In her view, words beget, create, indicate values; poets are sacred because they manipulate, manage, attend and offer conduits for messages, spin 'the rare intangible thread/ that binds all humanity/ to ancient wisdom', which is, of course, the ultimate good/god/goal (CP, p.523).

A rich reading by Susan Gubar traces the many

imagistic projections of quest for meaning through specifically female transformative power, including the seashell producing a pearl, the worm in a cocoon, the urn with its seed, the cartouche with its word, and the 'little boxes' which hatch butterflies. These make statements about pregnancy and birth, 'female sexuality and motherhood' which, all together, 'demonstrate the need for imagistic and lexical redefinition, an activity closely associated with the recovery of female myths. . .'.[27]

Friedman emphasises (as does Gubar's study) the revisionary nature of this work, in compelling dialogue with such representatives of patriarchal vision as John (of Revelations) and Freud. H.D.'s 'spiritual realism' counters Freud's 'materialist epistemology', not by opposition but by a dialogic movement of incorporation and transcending (*Psyche Reborn*, pp.102,107). H.D.'s revaluative probing of the maternal, fertility goddesses, a major scrutiny of a good or god (by one name, Venus) thought to be baleful, impure, lascivious, poisonous, reposes this culturally despised icon into the shrine provided by intellectual and emotional work done by the poet.

In 'The Walls Do Not Fall' as well, there is a growing affirmation, which builds slowly in the course of the section, of the maternal fertility and regenerative goddess present and secretly animating the proceedings. This begins the shift of weight which all three sections together accomplish by delegitimating the dominant narrative of patriarchal gods, reaffirming the muted narrative of female gods (in 'Tribute to the Angels') and finally rebalancing the religious and prophetic tradition between the genders in 'The Flowering of the Rod'.[28] For H.D. is an anti-patriarchal symbolist; her yearning for centre and presence still rupture the unspoken attachment, in most symbolist poetic practice, to a phallocentric focus.

Religion, art and medicine are each present as units of thought, image and argument, insistently, on all scales, in all places. The triple arts are first presented separately, component by component: the caduceus, or healing (I, section 3), the shell, or art (I, section 4), and the Mage, or religion (I, section 5). The three picto-graphic symbols to which the three sections can be, so to speak, reduced: the spiral, the jar/bud/wing/seed, and the rod are also the visual components of a caduceus, which is itself a symbol variously of religion (Hermes carries it), healing (physicians use it as emblem) and hermetic art, the stylus of spiritual realism. These three components can be traced throughout. Indeed, permuta-tions of these triple visual components will animate not only 'The Walls Do Not Fall' but its two companion poems as well.

The potent symbols, images and structures of the poem make many manifests of the patterns of conviction underlying visualisation: presence, mystery, access to a permanent store of knowledge. The snakes, the wavy hair, all the spirals heal. The rod, tree or rood regenerates, and resurrects. The flower, lily-bud, the little jar of perfume, are the fabricated essence of these necessities, or art. The caduceus-sign of the triple scientia, which is the sum total of all three (snake, tree, bud), is made and remade, found and refound in the argument of the poem.

'The Walls Do Not Fall' uses this caducean 'tripod' of healing, religion and art as an outline for poetic development. The sections on Osiris/Amen/Ra and the 'disentangling' and reweaving of religious imagery (sections 16-23) precede a set of sections (24-9) about stars/jars/boxes of 'that indisputable/ and absolute Healer, Apothecary', incidentally due to sprout into a fertile Mother Goddess tree (CP, pp.528-9). These are followed by H.D.'s amazingly pointed self-criticism of her art of poetry, which offers a most comprehensive and intelligent review of her own stylistic traits (sections 30–6), which she finds are necessitated by her project: the revaluing of a hoard of myths, and her tactic of 'spiritual realism' (CP, p.537). After this critical section, she offers a positive assessment of her poetics: it can offer critique, the establishment of parallel between history and myth, a mediation between individual and collective histories, and the 'hatching' or decoding of the cryptogram of each and every word (sections 37–40).

The hatching process of art leads back to the other elements of the 'tripod vision'. The ability poetically to deconstruct words, as in the set of Osiris phonemes (sections 40–3) leads to spiritual, even mystical knowledge of the One, and returns us to seeds (as in section 41). So the triple good is affirmed and reaffirmed; whichever way one looks healing comes from art/ religion; spiritual reality infuses art and healing (and so forth).

The Osiris phonemes offer a paradigmatic rune from ruin. H.D. will typically use a punning metonymic chain of connections (absolute poison to her detractors) to 'get over' dominant language. What may be said to happen when words are thus opened? First, in breaking words into their associative compounds ('Osiris'/'zrr-hiss' [CP, pp.540,542]), H.D. represents that apparently unconnected eras of history (Egypt/London) and opposing forces (regenerated fragments and destruction) are connected the deeper one tunnels. With this forthright association, words are then seen as the seeds of compacted understanding. The process of decoding reiterates the Osirian fragmentation. To achieve the Isisan rejuvenation, one must look hard at/for the scattered 'members' (syllables, associations) and understand the meanings offered by the fragmentation. Finally, such phonemic punning gives access to the language 'inside' the language, suggestively occult; suggestively female.[29]

True to the triple 'tripod pattern', each of the three epiphanies of Mary in 'Tribute to the Angels' produces or affirms one of the three scientia: healing, religion, art. The pulsing jewel with its iridescent changeable colours in the bottom of the crucible is the figure related to the sciences of alchemy and then medicine, a reinterpreted understanding of the crude, poisonous Venus. The Mary incarnating the May apple flower is the Mary of religion, a rod or rood. And clearly a Mary not as 'the painters' saw her but described anew by a visionary poet is the Mary of art. Each of these Marys is, or carries, one of the emblematic parts of a caduceus: a rod, a quivering jewel, and a blank-bud book with its 'tale of a jar or jars' (CP, p.571).

As the throbbing opalescent jewel, living and perfumed, found by alchemical fusion, its fragrance and shape suggest a milk-filled breast: not only an object of sight, but of physical touch. H.D. focuses her meditation on this jewel, setting words aside, neither naming nor thinking. This symbolic matter suggests it is an anti-bomb: an implosion which shows the same colours and vibrancy as an actual explosion, but to opposite intent, thus an answer to the male serpent Typhoon, god of war.[30] As the flowering may apple from a bomb-charred tree in a vacant lot, Mary is the principle of blossoming incarnate in the damaged historical time after the London Blitz. Again beyond verbalising, more like music, the presentation H.D. makes of this flowered rod is reminiscent of the high revelation of the Eleusinian Mysteries.

The vision of the Lady with her blank book, the third

irruption of a mother goddess, the third break in her well-planned narrative celebrating male angels, is a climactic moment of the whole poem because of H.D.'s critique of culture and of poetic stance. Her Mary, as she says, cannot be described citing or conforming to previous iconography. Indeed, the unwritten element of Mary and the unwritten status of her book are powerful statements of female authority. A catalogue (in sections 29–32, then 36–41) of the multifarious depictions of the Madonna in painting, icon and religious doctrine is interspersed with such comments as 'But none of these, none of these/ suggest her as I saw her. . .' and 'she bore/ none of her usual attributes; the Child was not with her' (CP, pp.566–7). Recall that none of the epiphanies uses metaphors of words (one is silent meditation, the next music, the third a blank book): this transcendence of poetry-as-usual has both a spiritual and a feminist dimension.

This new lady 'carries a book but it is not/ the tome of the ancient wisdom,// The pages, I imagine, are the blank pages/ of the unwritten volume of the new. . .' (CP, p.570). H.D.'s blank page of the new is a resistant exploration of the cultural imagery of woman as page awaiting someone else's writing.[31] Because Mary carries a book, not a baby, H.D. proposes the female authority of scribe and lawgiver, but unlike the Sibyl 'shut up in a cave', it is not a law in collaboration with (Roman) patriarchy. H.D. offers the possibility that Mary is not a conduit for One whom she bore, but is herself the One: the goddess is God. Further, a woman offers a participatory textual plurality, the virginal page is not single, hieratic, authoritarian revelation. It is the book of prophecy that does not look like a conventional book, from a prophet who does not act like a conventional prophet.

This section, using many small citations from and allusions to Revelations is a proud reconsideration of the absolutism and possessiveness of the prophetic stance. In a parallel to the injunction 'Thou shalt have no other gods before me', John insists that there be no prophets after him. His curse on additions and further witnessing is boldly opposed to the word of Christ who says, 'I make all things new'. H.D. creates a narrative in which the misogynist prophet is proved wrong by both the 'feminine god' and and female prophet.[32]

So in her use of John, H.D. is refabricating not only a misogynist tradition in its casting the Mother Goddess as the enemy of heaven, but all authoritarian voices within that tradition which seal the book. The sealing of the book is a trope for the silencing of women; the blank book is, then, the whiteness of multiplicity, pluralism, and a Christian polytheism; it is the possibility of female gender authority and women's speech.

If *Trilogy* II effects a displacement of the male principle (in prophet and angel) by a foregrounding of the female principle, the question that will animate *Trilogy* III concerns what to do with that male principle, where to put it, how to transform it. Indeed, across all three parts of the poem, patriarchal godhead has been changed respectively from father to son, from son to baby, from baby to sweet flowering bush. The *Logos* has become a veggie.

The third part of *Trilogy*, 'The Flowering of the Rod', offers another kind of critical narrative of female authority. H.D.'s story concerns two somewhat marginal characters in the Gospels, Kaspar the Mage, who brought myrrh as a gift to the Christ Child, and Mary Magdalene, the prostitute who figures as one of the Jesus company. H.D. proposes that, under the influence of joy at Christ's Epiphany, Kaspar had vowed, but then forgotten, to give Him a second jar of myrrh. Years pass; Mary Magdalene approaches him to purchase that myrrh so she can use it to anoint Christ at the Last Supper. In the explicit gender struggle between Kaspar's dismissive rejection and Magdalene's stubborn persistence, she is the vehicle through which his vow is fulfilled.

The replacement of a dominant Gospel narrative with two unrelated mentions of myrrh and with an occult and muted narrative 'not on record' is a move of critical reassessment. The relation H.D. creates between the protagonists casts many of the issues in gender terms. The precious balm itself is distilled by a group described as a male club, all processes and arrangements made to exclude women from medicine's mysterious arts. Indeed, Mary Magdalene is called mara (bitter Mary) because she has been excluded specifically by the tradition that myrrh must be made by male craftspeople because 'no secret was safe with a woman' (CP, p.589). Myrrh, the very substance of 'tripod' powers – a healing balm, a perfume, and a religious symbol – has been appropriated by males. Mary Magdalene's task (as Fast Mary of the Phallic Tower) is to break male hegemony: 'through my will and my power,/ Mary shall be myrrh' (CP, p.590).

Myrrh is continually affiliated with the sensual, with healing, and with a shift from bitterness to efflorescence and pleasure, a redefinition: '(though I am Mara, bitter) I shall be Mary-myrrh' (ibid., p.590). To rectify traditional exclusion of women, to make a mara-Mary become Mary-myrrh, the woman compels the Mage to acknowledge her power. Hence, the woman who seeks this myrrh is indecently assertive, 'unmaidenly', 'unseemly', not conformable to any gender codes. She deliberately shrugs off all the man's social cues demanding her inferiorisation or timidity. The encounter of the odd, defiant woman with the different Mage will make Kaspar the initiate, and Mary the priestess.

So the conversion of Kaspar is not incidental or accidental but speaks to H.D.'s central concerns. Under Mary's influence, in fact, looking at the light in her wavy, snaky hair, Kaspar has a great, saturating vision concerning lost goddesses, lost, utopian cities, and the primacy and power of the mother–child dyad (the fertility couplet) at the heart of the 'new' religion of Christ.

For 'The Flowering of the Rod' is designed like a butterfly: one might say a caduceus has given birth. One wing features Mary Magdalene and the 'sexism' of Kaspar; the sinuous centre is Mary's wavy hair let down at the Last Supper, which induces a secondary frisson of disgust in Simon, the host. The second wing is Kaspar's release into vision by this confrontation over the possession of myrrh. By this design, H.D. says insistently that both male and female vision are necessary for a transformed spiritual ideology. Female intellectual and emotional passion will precipitate a major spiritual change, as the snaky body will metamorphose into a butterfly, but both wings together, both liberated genders, will allow spiritual flight.

This statement of the conversion of a male seer by female pertinacity and by a vision generated by his contact with her is another transposition of H.D.'s analysis with Freud. That the climax of *Trilogy* is Kaspar's vision, made of pictures in light in a darkened room without any light source (see section 17) seems H.D.'s most teasing commentary on Freud's scepticism about the Corfu vision and its similar setting. In section 40, she even uses somewhat precise, quasi-scientific language ('spiritual optical-illusion'; 'proved mathematically'; 'refracted'; 'vibration'; 'vacuum') none of which is sufficient to explain what happened and how. The only sufficient explanation is social and spiritual: the Mage is marginal, he feels inadequate; he has made unspoken, almost forgotten, vows. Her presence releases Kaspar to his own memories of marginality and pain, so he ends by identifying with her and with the earth and fertility goddesses she incorporates instead of standing in political or intellectual confrontation against her. Mary has 'cured' and thus converted Kaspar to what H.D. said, commenting to Freud, was 'an unusual way to think' (through visions, reveries, hallucinations), but not, she also says in every tone and gesture, an inadequate way to think. In fact, quite the opposite.

H.D. even gives Freud-in-Kaspar the engendered spiritual vision that makes a commentary on the work on which he was engaged during their contact: Moses and monotheism is countered by Mary and polytheism. The so-called demons apparently 'cast out' of Magdalene come back as daimons of fertility, in a stunning retelling of the Scriptures. Similarly, the flowering rod – a branch of myrrh, the caduceus, Christ Himself – is a corrective of tradition for it returns the phallic symbolic patterns to their female origins. Myrrh can now be distilled by women; the caduceus has been reformulated by a woman and the snake, rod and bud have all been returned to their maternal meanings. Finally, the 'thing' held in the arms of Bona Dea at the end of *Trilogy* is not the 'Mosaic' male baby but the flower or sheaf of wheat that particular fertility goddess carries: in this case, myrrh.

So the secret quest in this poem is to bring two jars of myrrh (healing balm) to two forms of myrrh (Christ and Mary) who are, as reborn son and Great Mother, one manifestation of fertility and power. It is, thus, almost tautological: 'the same – different – the same attributes,/ different yet the same as before' (CP, p.571). This is, of course, a version of Christianity: some *dramatis personae*, some theology, and some structures of solace are familiar. H.D. is a sympathetic believer in at least resurrection and incarnation. But this mother–baby matrix is hardly the Christianity of Father–Son–Holy Ghost; it is, in short, different not the same as before, and critical of the unreservedly patriarchal cast of some versions of that faith. If God is at least a nurturer (*Trilogy* I) at most he is a woman (*Trilogy* II) and finally a synthesis: mother–son, or Mary–myrrh.

In the notes on Chapter I of *The Gift*, H.D. startlingly, provocatively says that her uncle Fred Wolle's simple vocal rendition of the 'Ballad of the Four Marys', accompanied by H.D.'s mother, was more meaningful to her than his conducting of Bach's *St Matthew's Passion*.[33] She counterposes the magisterial and acclaimed work about the death of Christ by a renowned male composer with the anonymous work in a woman's voice about female guilt and suffering. Like Woolf's subtle use of the same ballad in *A Room of One's Own*, this is a statement of allegiance to the maternal line of artists and, for H.D., of visionaries which in her own family she can trace back to Mamalie's grandmother, a woman named Mary. And, as one Mary says in *Trilogy*, 'O, there are Marys a-plenty' – at least three and possibly a fourth (CP, p.590). There is Mary/Psyche who is the butterfly out of her cocoon; there is Mary Magdalene, hero/ine of the final book, who is 'Mara' but will become 'Mary-myrrh'; finally, Mary Madonna, a figure closer to Bona Dea, is the climactic sight. The fourth Mary is of course, H.D., singer and watcher, like the witness to a Mosaic story in the other Testament. The relevance of this Mary, Miriam, is sharpened when one remembers an important passage in *Tribute to Freud*. The poet and the therapist had rather different interpretations of a significant 'dream of an Egyptian Princess': Freud's that H.D. wanted to become baby Moses, substituting her womanhood for a manhood because of female lack. H.D. implies, that she wants to be, that she is, Miriam, accepting womanhood and its authority. As singer, prophet, dancer, seer Miriam accumulates a generative female authority; it is a live priestess who speaks.

As *Helen in Egypt* will have a 'coda' in 'Winter Love', so *Trilogy* has a coda in 'Sagesse', a spiritual poem from the post-war period (written 1957). It too will counter the scepticism of a psychoanalyst (Erich Heydt), using him as the emblem of major cultural materials and systems, and creating a subversive, critical writing that counters his assumptions.

If one looks at the full page of *The Listener* upon which the frightened owl, inspiration of 'Sagesse', flares out its wings like great horns turned downward, it appears that the daimon of Woolf's *Three Guineas*, with its devastating pictures of male authority, hovers over this enterprise.[34] The news montage on that page presents photographs of bowler-hatted gentlemen, diplomats and heads of state; there are photos of solemn men watching a cricket match. And there is a bizarre shot of a male sculptor finishing up a bare-breasted female wooden figurehead for a ship, the female sculpture bound by a rope, hanging in his studio. These three pictures of complacency and national/sexual politics as usual are joined by two photos from another region of fear and resistance. There are early protesters against the hydrogen bomb and nuclear war, wearing hoods like bomb tails masking their faces, recalling that H.D. was stunned by the use of atomic power as firepower in warfare. And there is a close-up of a feather-fanning, startled owl, recent acquisition at the

London Zoo. The owl becomes a symbol of linked patterns of fear, marginality and resistance: fear of normal politics, fear of a third world war (which H.D. felt strongly), fear of gender relations, and the greater wisdom that comes from marginality.

That owl becomes a mark of shattered powers for both the poet and her double, a sensitive working-class girl who had survived the Blitz. In her use of dialect, of conversation and her clear thematic statements about the bravery of the common people, H.D. is embedding a dear truth, newly-illuminated, rescued from banality: *vox populi* is *vox dei*. In trying to meditate upon and collect the outcasts, including herself, now old, pained and insomniac, she turns her nervous isolation to deepened understanding through the thematic and structural use of angels, just as she had done in 'Tribute to the Angels'.

Depending on a work of spiritual guidance which assigns a guardian or responsible angel, round the clock, every twenty minutes, H.D. cites and plays allusively with these apparently exotic chronometrical presences. This use of the angels simply grounds the poem in a quickened, quickening reading of signs, a series of correspondences between her feelings and memories and their powers. As vulnerability and responsive caring are incarnate in each moment with its protector, so too a caring force and wounded vulnerability, incarnate eveywhere, is the constant sign of God. When her tactic of combining 'hieratic rhythm, then the most ordinary association' is questioned by one of the imbedded critics or detractors of her last poems (in this case 'Germain', or Erich Heydt), the poet responds, 'isn't that the whole point, anyway?'[35]

Chapter Four

'Desire Begets Love'

She knows . . . that 'women are individually seeking, as one
woman, fragments of the Eternal Lover'. As the Eternal
Lover has been scattered or disassociated, so she, in her
search for him. . . . She seeks him in fantasy, myth. She has
found him, of course. But she can not yet correlate or relate
the various entities that make up her own fragments,
though in Egypt they were related for her; the formula was
presented. . . . She knows that to keep him, she must lose
him. She does not know how she knows this. But the seal is
set on her knowledge. She can not know that she knows
this, until she has progressively retraced her steps,
redeemed not so much the fragments of Osiris, as of his
sister, twin or double, the drowned or submerged Isis.
 This Isis takes many forms, as does Osiris.

(*Notes on Recent Writing*), (1949), pp. 4–5)[1]

In a significant passage in 'Professions for Women',
Virgina Woolf traces the repetitive struggle of the
woman writer for the authority to write, that is, to

101

transcend (and to mend the damage of) the feminine. One part of this struggle involves 'killing the angel in the house', a provocatively blasphemous conjuncture.[2] The angel's maternal conservatism restricts boldness, judgement, and outspokenness. The repression of any desire, want or need and the repression of sexualities are mutually buttressing substructures in the larger issues of female authority. As is well known, Woolf confesses that despite *Orlando*, she has had the most trouble achieving permission to depict sexuality in art. The erotic and the sexual are relatively fraught arenas in which to establish female authority because it is risky for a woman writer to insist upon and examine that force by which women have been taxed, and about which cultural ambivalence and blame have accrued. Sexuality exposes a woman writer to speculation; it touches on many taboos, and its use in a text can be subject to disparaging, even insulting, autobiographical readings.

The presence of desire and the erotic defines the final phase of H.D.'s literary career, from 1949 to 1961. After her self-exploratory *Notes on Recent Writing* (1949), and throughout the last decade of her life, beginning when she was well over sixty years old, she experiments with placing various kinds of female desire (sexual/erotic, maternal) at the heart of narrative and language – in the production of texts and in the analysis of culture. In treating sexualities in an autobiographical fashion, H.D. claims a consummate gender authority: to speak of female sexuality from a personal centre, to consider sexuality as part of her identity, to play with forms, stages, forces and structures of sexuality, and to reread the role of sexuality in history. In so doing, she plays with fantasies, with the fictive and with the frank, including fictive frankness, frank fantasies, fantastic fictions.

In 1949, in the aftermath of the relationship of (one-sided) thraldom which involved Hugh Dowding, Air Marshall during the Battle of Britain, and in the aftermath of a serious post-war breakdown in 1946, H.D. proposes some patterns in her use of heterosexual romance. There are two stages related to the male figure: affiliation or access and then renunciation or sacrifice. This, in itself, is not especially unusual (nor even unfeminine).[3] But, in *Notes on Recent Writing*, she goes on to show that romance is more than a personal daydream; it is a 'speech or language' of outcast, exotic, marginal and heterodox peoples, whose articulation of desire is more than 'self-expression' but also 'world-expression' (NRW, p.58). This bold concept of the erotic played out for spiritual stakes on an historical terrain enlarged it far beyond the domesticity of depicted relationships, acceptable or taboo. After her final portrait of domestic ties (in *Bid Me to Live*, completed in 1949), she will henceforward cast the erotic onto a vaster screen. This kind of development is illustrated by a subtle letter (1934) to her close friend and possibly her lover, Sylvia Dobson, who was clearly nervous about being pinned and pegged, catalogued or categorised by psychoanalysis: 'It is hardly a question of your being, as you say, A2 or B3 Lesbian. . . . But it's a matter of something infinitely bigger than Lesbian A2 or anything. The Lesbian or the homo-sexual content is only a symbol – note, I did not say a "symptom". *That* is not very important. *How* you love is more important than WHO you love.'[4]

The assumption of erotic authority involved articulating desire for males, assessment of her desire to be a desired woman, a critical and revisionary reading of the role of erotic desire within culturally paradigmatic materials, e.g. the Trojan War. This is the desire of Isis for Osiris. But the epigraph alludes to another, matching desire: of Isis for Isis. The feminine quest for the Lover (*pace* Pearson ['Interview', p.445]) is not the more prominent; H.D. places the heterosexual, culturally powerful script in a new context, one formed by the reconstruction of Isis in two forms. First, as the sister-mirror; And second as the Great Mother. For in late H.D., there is some encoded acknowledgement of lesbian and/or sisterly ties, and there is a pronounced matrisexuality in mother–child relations from the perspective of child and of mother both. Here vulnerability and protection have an erotic depth; here the 'child' is, as well, an avatar of a new age–Eros reborn.

Bid Me to Live, among the very last of her published works (1960), has a curious status in H.D.'s career as it spans the four periods here delineated. It reflects materials like 'Eurydice' from the struggle for cultural authority; it is an assemblage from 'Madrigal cycle' materials of the 1920s; it was provoked back into life by her analysis with Freud. Its completion in 1949 opens the questions of erotic authority, and the fourth phase.

Bid Me to Live discusses the struggle of the woman poet against manifold denials of her authority in the context of emotional and sexual entanglements on the home front during World War I. Julia's husband and her spiritual mentor respectively (Rafe and Rico, based on Aldington and Lawrence) engage in games of power, desire, withdrawal and rejection, centring on Julia's capacities, notably her sexuality after a stillbirth, and her sense of exposure, of being 'jeered at' for her writing (BMTL, p.164). Aside from their specific sniping at her ego strength, her sexual and maternal capacities, and her artistic tactics, the men with whom she is involved seem to erode her particularity as intact and unique self. In one case she 'was to be used' to 'feed the flame of Rico'; in the other 'she and Bella [Rafe's florid mistress] were simply abstractions, were women of the period, were WOMAN of the period, the same one' (BMTL, pp.88, 103).

Personal and political situations elide; Julia feels 'gassed' (as the soldiers were) by the residue of poison in Rafe's lungs brought into their house directly from the front. As a token of these war-borne changes, the very room she called hers 'was no longer her home, her own; strange cross-currents had been at work upon it' (ibid., p.85). The intact space as if the core of the self, so vital to women seeking artistic presence had become 'a public highway' (ibid., p.85). Because public and private space are fundamentally altered ('as the war crept closer, as it absorbed everything'), so H.D. makes Julia's job of reconstructing the damaged self in love and work have a political dimension as well as a personal. Like Woolf's *Three Guineas*, this work studies, in its own way, the continuities between private house and public realm.

Julia's writing is a battleground, for even her most private communications – letters to the front, rough drafts of poems – are compromised by the private war between the sexes, a colonial takeover which she appears to be losing. She is criticised by Rico for her scope, and challenged to curtail her production of a poem of revisionary mythmaking to that which she is supposed to know best – Eurydice alone, 'the woman vibration' (BMTL, p.51). And she is riled by Rafe for daring in certain rough drafts to write 'clichés' – as if even one's drafts had to be perfect, finished works. So she writes false rough drafts to include mentions of 'forthcoming' poems in letters to Rafe, as if her poetic production could compensate him for some of the horrors of trench warfare and stalemate. In short, her writing is (whether praised or hectored) possessed by others, and is not autonomous but functioning variously in others' literary and gender schemes.

So the problematic of this novel corresponds to H.D.'s first phase, her desires for cultural authority. With the help of a modest and unassuming lover, with the 'space and time' Vane ceremoniously provides, with 'a room to work in', she begins to write – translating Greek, writing definitive letters of adieu to Rico. Finally 'flamboyantly ambitious . . . she wanted to coin new words' (BMTL, pp.157, 161, 162, 163). And she postulates a male liberator from these sexual battles.

But, reflecting H.D.'s concerns after her analysis and after her survival of the Blitz, other issues besides the cultural authority of gender become central. Past mid-book, at the turning point, Julia claims the risky right of exposure and, rather than taking cover in the basement of her boarding-house, she steps, with Vane, into a London night at the very time of the Zeppelin raids. (This recurrent gesture of H.D.'s later works, of the ultimate test on a female quest being the exposure to fire, to bomb, to warfare, is explored as well in *The Gift*.) With some telling, floating remarks (so akin to Woolf's practice in *The Years*), 'This show, this particular show is over' and 'I think people are beginning to come to . . . a door opened', H.D. underscores that spiritual change for which she and her hero/ines are ceaselessly to work in her post-World War II writings (BMTL, p.113).

The social dilemmas of the khaki mass, and the patriarchal personality which is its root cause are the political problematics which complement the toils of romantic thraldom and cultural authority which the book certainly addresses. *Bid Me to Live* and its study of the rupture of coequal genders because of the masculinist values derived from war exemplifies the consideration of militarism which is a unifying theme in H.D.'s work as a whole: in *Asphodel* (with its tracing of the effects of war on a male poet); in *Palimpsest* (tracing the effects of war on a female poet); in *Trilogy* (the fusing of shards after the bombing of London); in *The Gift* (fratricidal civil and colonial wars in America; civilian vulnerability in the Blitz); in *Helen in Egypt* (Achilles and the Iron-Ring, the Command, as fascism reprojected); in *Tribute to Freud* (Nazism and official terror with its personal meanings).

Like the toast to the new world centrally positioned in *The Years* after the same Zeppelin raids of World War I, *Bid Me to Live* presents some kind of ineffable hope, embodied in a female goddess – a benevolent vision of female beauty achieved through cinema – to intervene on deep and saturated levels in the politics of the unconscious. For a female goddess of fertility and thus hope seems to reign over the hoard of singing soldiers in a theatre.

A fecund series of meditations on film and the politics of narrative in *Close Up* can gloss the importance of this turning-point in the cinema with Julia transfixed by the image of Garbo on the screen.[5] H.D.'s studies in *Close Up* often contrast various conventional plots – melodrama, 'vapid romance' – and the tacky 'showgirls' who soon inhabited dominant cinema with the potential cinema had to present 'classic, ancient Beauty'.[6] H.D. took cinema very seriously, comparing it to the mysteries at Delphi or Eleusis because the state in which one viewed it seemed to evoke a different from normal layer of consciousness. Because this layer was universal, cinema had a political potential for rescripting ideologies at a site beneath dominant narratives. And as well it was a psychic instrument, giving an individual access to a state of initiation, or spiritual fulfilment in a realm under the ego. Two tendencies in cinema practice – between becoming 'dope' and aphrodisiac or 'spiritual' and 'intellectual stimulus' – were revealed especially in gender issues and in the representation of women. In her analysis of the bodies and the images of the desired: stars, often women, H.D. protests against the passive pleasure of the viewer, and at the same time understands the desire for 'healing in blur of half tones and hypnotic vibrant darkness'.[7] H.D. wants the massive iconisation of figures of desired women in cinema to be focused, not by a cheapening titillation, but by an enriching access to grave images of female power mediated by erotic yearning.

These concerns for social conversion by the impact of desire for female beauty, and the special status of a female 'see-er' in decoding hieroglyphs which reveal these issues are directly visible in *Helen in Egypt*, a magisterial long poem (1952–55/1961 pub.) (BMTL, p.146). Where to 'place' erotics, the erotic female and her cultural meaning, is certainly a question that can be asked about Helen of Troy, as about virtually no other figure in Western literature. H.D. undertakes a major task of cultural recuperation in her deconstructed 'epic' to reconstruct not so much a new Helen, but the oldest and 'therefore' truest Helen, a measured displacement of the narrative of war.[8]

Helen in Egypt was written in three almost equal sections, of 7, 7, then 6 Books each, each book with eight poems in an unrhymed *terza rima*, these poems introduced with mysterious prose passages of summary and rumination, in the poet's voice, as the poems seem to be in Helen's. The three divisions – 'Pallinode' (defence or apology), 'Leuké' (white island) and 'Eidolon' (little icon/image) sum up a stance toward this story: an explanatory revision of Helen, a space like a blank page of incipience, the fertile space in which memory is activated, and the third inscription of some impacted cocoon of *material*, the mark that marks all: Helen/ Thetis[9]

Helen is both 'writer', reader and main character a curious status which has at least one theoretical effect–of collapsing subject–object distinctions between the thing scrutinised and the viewer. For the main character to be a frank projection of H.D. herself – while bearing so interestingly her own mother's given name – and for a female character to be a serious reader of her own desires ('I am instructed, I know the script'), not an object or symbol of desire for others starkly cedes from a number of the conventions of poetic depiction.[10]

So a primary refusal of *Helen in Egypt* is of the woman as spectacle upon which, as contemporary feminist film criticism eloquently reminds us, much of Western conventions of representation depend: woman as body, woman as desired object, woman as quintessentially sexual. All this may be summed up in one myth of ultimate Beauty and transgressive desire: Helen of Troy.[11] Instead of being the 'captive and absent', hated, yet passive Helen of H.D.'s short lyric poem, this Helen is a site of resistance by being plural (offering a contradictory Helen to both former lovers Paris and Achilles) and palimpsestic, as a series of eras overlayer and are read in relation. She is the object of scrimming (a Veil figures heavily) and scriving (different picture writings, like hieroglyphics and zodiacs, figure also); she is the subject (reader of her own text). The poem even writes across culture by situating Helen in the 'wrong' place, not Troy but Egypt (following several non-Homeric traditions).[12] The poem allows icon to become critic, yet remain icon; object to become subject, yet remain object; interpeted to become interpreter, yet remain interpreted.

Helen's major activity is decoding and remembering: decoding the Amen-script in a temple very like Karnak (site of one of H.D.'s visionary experiences); decoding two hieroglyphs. One is the 'bird' of Isis, the other is nenuphar or water lily, which in this poem alludes to the Great Mother with child, around which all other petals are arranged in a 'subtle genealogy' that serves various biographical and cultural functions in H.D.'s *oeuvre*. She also decodes both Zodiac and 'eidolon', pictorial visualisations of some prime reality about which the poem can certainly be opaque.

And she decodes her own memories under the tutelage of Theseus and remembers in such a way that a tapestry of mind is rewoven, a cocoon of nurturance is accepted and therefore an identity (Psyche, the butterfly) emergent. In an important reading which traces the centrality to the poem of H.D.–Freud analysis, Susan Friedman argues that Helen's tasks are psychoanalytic: 'to clarify her relation to the hated phantom of Helen, and to recover the significance of fragmented memory' (Friedman, *Psyche Reborn*, p.60). Friedman emphasises that the whole narrative is a quest or 'psychoanalytic epic' in which Helen interprets her mysterious pictorial memories – recurrent visual images that haunt her – such as a fluttering veil or the sight of her deserted child's staring eyes (ibid., p.66). Thus the 'action' of the poem is the 'reading' of these picture-memories and the healing that occurs when they are encompassed and understood.

So *Helen in Egypt* can be read as a quest for wholeness and integration of a self whose many polarities fuse in the psychoanalytic crucible. Or it can be read as an acceptance of the ever unravelling and reconstituting of a subject-in-process/ subject-in-question. The latter is symptomatically indicated (as Carolyn Burke argues about other writers) by issues about naming, such as

H.D.'s pseudonyms and plays with her own name, multiple uses of her initials, and the constant appearance of a subject-in-narrative who both is and is not the author as ego.[13] Using Julia Kristeva, Burke debates how to read the 'I' in women's poetry, asking whether it must always be the self in a confessional mode, or whether it is not as plausibly a self-conscious producer of and commentator upon discourse and her positions within it. In short, is the speaker a 'self' (whole, homogeneous, or seeking wholeness/identity, transcendence), or may a speaker be a 'subject' (naming her place in and absences from registers of language and culture). H.D.'s combination of a female thematics and certain experimentalist language strategies make either interpretation plausible, and both together (even in their contradictions) vital.

The extremely peculiar and unsettling space/voice which this poem creates may begin to be comprehended in view of its radical gestures toward consciousness and its thematics of the maternal. Is this a space of memory or event? Is it a space of desire or death – an active world, or a posthumous world, the whole like the obligatory one-book trip to the underworld in epics. Are the characters mimetic, or are they projections; does the narrative 'progress' or repeat? All these options prove superficial, not to say irrelevantly dichotomised, in the new space and 'new spirit-order' of plural ghosts all entering an ultimate maternal space: an 'epic' deconstructed because it is the 'epic' of 'chora' (HE, p.217). Despite these considerations, and despite H.D.'s contention that she was writing a book for adepts (probably because she included oblique versions of her encounters with and spirit messages from the dead), the essential points of *Helen in Egypt* are clear.

In *Helen in Egypt*, *The Iliad*, given its status as

approximate source, is treated rather offhandedly. H.D. makes a two-line allusion, virtually lost in this lengthy text, to deny the central event of that other story: 'Achilles skulks in his tent,/ they said, but it was not true . . . ' (HE, p.247). In her version, he was on the beach, fondling the icon of his mother. H.D. gives a summary of the whole issue of causation: 'Helen of Troy was a phantom. . . . The Greeks and the Trojans alike fought for an illusion' (ibid., p.1). She dismisses the culturally reiterative process of telling and retelling that story: 'The script was a snare' (ibid., p.220). By these kinds of remarks, H.D. constructs a large area of marginality in apparently studied indifference to direct confrontation with 'culture as it is', which, by its own force, poetic elegance and pertinacity of approach (what H.D. called her 'stubbornness'), creates another 'side' to the library, a spacious and knowing side which attempts a complete explanatory system (e.g. for war, misogyny, sexuality) to displace culturally prevalent interpretations. Epic is alluded to, but H.D. floods epic with otherness; univocal narrative sequence is alluded to, but also flooded with its undoing in questions posed in prose headnotes.[14] All the doubling and undoing of events, all intricacies and even unintelligibilities may yet be reduced to one or two words

> 'Isis', he said, 'or Thetis', I said,
> recalling, remembering, invoking
> his sea-mother . . .
>
> (HE, p.14)

Spoken at the beginning, this radically removes the necessity for sequential revelation from the narrative.

H.D.'s argument about the myth is, however, more subtle than a denial of Helen's role in the war by the mechanism of her transport to Egypt. The myth is not

112

reversed; Helen is not innocent as charged. It is delegitimated by ruptures of sequence and especially causality; that rupture is explicitly revisionary of the impact of female guilt. Beginning the argument with a denial of Helen's role, the mysterious revelations refabricate the myth in a new way by exploring the ways Helen as Love in fact helps to cause the war, but also cure it. The process as Susan Friedman outlines it is: a study of the negative identity of Helen in dominant culture; her re-entrance into memory and the recovery of the past; her understanding of the ceaseless dialectic of love and strife; her revisionary understanding of the feminine in its associations with fertility, peace, order; her grief for other women sacrificed to the masculine 'warrior cult'; and finally, the way love/the Goddess works through Helen to challenge Achilles' allegiance to the 'Iron-Ring' of a proto-fascist hierarchy (Friedman, *Psyche Reborn*, pp.256–67).

Thus the fusion of contradictory aspects of Helen's history are constantly proposed: not just a both/and of dualisms overcome, but a triple play of both/and/*and*:

> Helen in Egypt,
> Helen at home,
> Helen in Hellas forever.
> (HE, p. 190)

H.D.'s consistent use of antiquity, and the intensified interest that marks *Helen in Egypt* occurs as a desire to revamp a historical conjuncture: a point at which Western mind and idea patterns were made and set. H.D.'s poetic history of consciousness traces the way Egypt – a symbol of the mother and therefore of fusion, incest, desire and death – has been tampered with and displaced from our understanding, replaced by the

113

Graeco-Roman civilisation: the father, differentiation, violence (including rape and war), repression, The Command, and laws by which male power exercises itself to control death. To constitute itself, Western civilisation has made an 'exodus from Egypt'.[15] H.D. wants to replace that bellicose father–civilisation with Hellas, the mother.

Helen in Egypt seriously intends itself as an anti-war text, which uses an examination of the roots of violence in repression of love of the mother to propose an alternative: lyre for 'bowman's arc' and 'a rhythm as yet unheard,/ to challenge the trumpet-note' (HE, pp.230, 229). The rupture of story, the 'thoughts too deep to remember,/ that break through the legend' and signal the delegitimation of the old Helen of Troy story of 'fame' and 'beauty', replacing these with the male 'new Mortal' and the female 'psyche' compound of Helen/Thetis – these are thoughts of the mother (ibid., pp.258–9, 10).

Through *Helen in Egypt*, H.D. shows that all desire is matrisexual; that all polarities, including major oppositional conflicts (love and death, eros and conflict), can be sublated through the mother; and finally that all forms of anger and rejection occur for imperfect recognitions of this fact.

> I [Helen, imagining Achilles' thoughts]
>   knew he loved, that I knew
> the ecstasy of desire had smitten him,
> burnt him; touched with the Phoenix-fire,
>
> the invincible armour
> melted him quite away,
> till he knew his mother;

The word 'knew' challenges us with shadow stories of, allusions to, incest which flicker through this tale. That the next line is 'but he challenged her, beat her back' only returns us to the initiatory moment of male assault and rejection prior to induction into a mystery (ibid., p.261).

All male violence is an incomplete, culturally damaging turn from unaccepted maternal love and power and, by extension, from the life-force of the Great Goddess. Especially aggressive sexuality functions as a second-rank cover story for this original passion. All kinds of contemptuous challenge and assault, all expressions of sexual hatred, desire to hurt women, H.D. shows are a shamed avoidance for an almost unspeakable depth of passionate attraction for the mother.

> He could name Helena,
> but the other [Thetis] he could not name;
> she was a lure, a light,
>
> an intimate flame, a secret kept
> even from his slaves, the elect,
> the innermost hierarchy;
>
> only Helena could be named
> and she was a public scandal.
>
> (HE, p.251)

Yet the 'Love Goddess' is shown to be an expression of the Great Mother, and hence fundamental erotics are matrisexual. The 'dart of Love/ is the dart of Death' (ibid., p.303) not only because of erotic piercings, like the arrow of Eros, but because through the mother, carnality and the mortal body (the 'Achilles heel') are born – a Dinnersteinian hypothesis after all.

In writing from an erotic/sensual, incestuous yearning for the mother and in then matching this matrisexual Eros with heterosexual passion, in claiming maternal love as the occulted element in our civilisation,

115

and heterosexuality as one specific version of it, H.D. took several risks. Unlike her critical rejection of icon status and her wary, yet fascinated teatment of sexuality in such work as *HERmione*, in the later poems, H.D. has the strength (of achievement), the stylised encounters with at least the male figures involved, the mantle of old age, and the interpretive structure about matrisexuality to help her regard, and make into art an overwhelming engagement/engorgement with heterosexual desire. From 1955 through her final poem in 1960, with focuses upon Erich Heydt, Ezra Pound and Lionel Durand, respectively, she explored sexual yearning and the powers of eros.[16] Her finding: erotics is a form of spiritual initiation into two mysteries: psychic communication and resurrection: 'desire begets love'.

A pattern of intense attraction, an induced and well-wrought erotics, occurs in the cluster of works treating her bond to Erich Heydt, an analyst and doctor at the Küsnacht Klinik (nursing home) where she went in 1953 for two operations, then chose, from 1953, to spend a number of years, using the setting as a convent or spiritual retreat (Guest, 1984, p.305). Not only an erotic and psychic attraction to Heydt, but also a maternal attraction to a younger patient offer the pretext for *Compassionate Friendship*, a memoir of H.D.'s writings, which situates them with various 'irrational' techniques of analysis, joining a female mind to a 'feminine' space of unconscious urges, pluralities, reversals. The technique of aligning different eras so that certain 'points' coincide, H.D. calls 'a correlation of entities' (CF, p.37). It is a way of establishing thick fictional networks among her friends and of transferring emotional charges across long-separated eras.

Setting up these relations and then decoding them had long been part of the meditative practice that contributed to H.D.'s writing. By the end of her life, H.D. had built on that tendency to make her 'super-imposition of place on place, of people on people' into a private historical, numerological and mystical process of reading her past life and works for prophecies of her current relationships and works (TT, p.9). Memory creates identity rather than the opposite: '[I] have woven myself into my present-self or protected my present with my writing, the recovery of the past . . .' (CF, p.65). She typically rephrases and reorganises the eras of her life in each memoir (increasingly with numerological notations, linking her history to the history of the world). In this memoir, for instance, she finds her life organised by seven-year cycles, each touching on one of seven stellar 'brothers' (among them D.H. Lawrence, Ezra Pound, Cecil Gray, Kenneth Macpherson, Walter Schmideberg – and now, Erich Heydt) as erotic or intellectual focal points (ibid., pp.88–90, 35).[17]

This writing is a form of interpretation for H.D., a way of reading the signs and signals given, a way of recalling or reinventing details, weighing them in context, studying their significances, and matching them with other materials. Sometimes overwhelmingly private, for fans only, sometimes brilliantly exemplary of female patterns, always the material is a Penelopean depiction: woven, unwoven, reconsidered, rewoven, a textile of thick meanings or a cocoon (to use H.D.'s major biological metaphor) of self-enclosure by self-disclosure[18]

H.D.'s process of living, recording, transposing, reading and reinterpreting, which incidentally makes her essay-memoirs a crucial genre for her *oeuvre* as a whole and a major contribution to female modernism, created a bio-biblioglyphic reverberation between her work and her life so intense that by her ruminative old

117

age, she felt that 'outside exists in a secondary dimension . . . everything outside can be lighted, renewed by this within' (CF, p.75). If consciousness and reality are transposed and revalued, so is chronological time. Those people who are especially valuable to her now – like Heydt, like Durand – have something in them that 'makes the past come true' (ibid, p.91).

One of the major interests of *Compassionate Friendship* is the insight given into her continuing practice of poetry. Both before sleeping, and after breakfast, she takes a 'meditation hour' in which she returns to the hypnogogic state of near dream. 'This state', she says with a shattering simplicity, 'is life to me' (ibid, p.92). She describes meditating on mystical texts, on numbers, circles, crosses: vision occurs, and she has 'Visitors' or significant, generative dreams (ibid., pp.66-7, 93).[19] After confessing this 'semi-trance', she becomes concerned (this memoir is surely written to the future) with a possible source of negative judgement on her authority. Hence she makes a special effort to assimilate her practice to that of a male master, W.B. Yeats, quoting with great approval his use of the term 'reverie' for exactly this state, and his use of the state to 'bring our souls to crisis' – not the crisis of a specific plot or action, but the crisis of 'passion' itself (ibid., p.93, from Yeats' *Autobiographies*). It is especially significant that she wants to bolster her practice by recalling his, given her subtle but pertinacious effort in her later works to construct interpretations of fellow poets (Ezra Pound, St-John Perse) which, while alluding to their mastery, shift their ground to hers.

This memoir is filled with the political 'paranoia' – H.D.'s own word – characteristic of the post-war period, but also characteristically personalised, as a version of the erotic 'paranoia' of psyche, palimpsest, prophecy. She registers in the tie to Heydt the potential for a 'vibration, intoxication in the air' which is both erotic and a way of heightening all intensities of feeling and understanding (CF. p.25). Her intense, overwrought readings of every event, her presentation of a whole Klinik, nurses, Sisters, patients and all, living out a collective transference to Heydt, her watching of his every movement, including his friends is an overinvestment not so much in sex *per se*, but, in a Foucaultean sense, in the discourse of confession and the rhetorics of those discourses: will to knowledge and elaboration of meanings; the interplay of powers and pleasures (powers of speaking, or being revealed, pleasures of listening, even a voyeuristic pleasure).[20] In her later life, as this memoir shows, H.D. had perfected her erotics; sexual feeling was directed toward the production and, as we shall see, critique of discourses of Eros which further revealed or claimed to reveal a path to spiritual illumination and 'integration' (CF, p. 68).

End to Torment and 'Winter Love' are linked works, one an autobiographical reflection in a daybook (March–July 1958), using the essayistic method of writing indebted to psychoanalysis. Random associative memories accrete, past and present situations overlap, allusive and indirect admissions are encoded (as if unconsciously) in imagery. She then becomes her own analyst, showing how all roads lead to central discoveries. The second is a poem begun six months later (January–April 1959) which invents the story of young Helen's passion for Odysseus to add to the myth hoard. Both works review, reinvent and reconsider H.D.'s early tie to Ezra Pound (1903–19). Both works use the risky root of sexuality and sexual desire.

Sexuality functions as a basic element for *End to Torment*. H.D. is infected again with a phallic romance by

Erich Heydt's medical injection simultaneous with a confessional injunction: to talk to him of Ezra Pound (ETT, p.11). She is wary and resistant but is slowly provoked in part by her complex attraction to Heydt, and by the atmosphere of empathetic interest created by her trans-Atlantic 'disciple', Norman Holmes Pearson, whose measured but fervent letters played so crucial a role in eliciting the works of her later years. Sexuality remains the cunning pretext and subtext at once in the interface created between Ezra and Erich and their phallic pressure. The memoir is the occasion in which she confesses to and recreates her sexual frustration after fifty years of half-arousal focused on Pound and offers a fictional solution.

In *End To Torment* H.D. engaged again with the contradictory positions for male–female ties (coequality and gender hierarchy) visible in Pound's *Hilda's Book* and replicated in *End to Torment*. One script which H.D. calls an 'uncoordinated entity' evokes the twins who are one being – male and female together, like the mystical Swedenborgean Seraphita–Seraphitus in the Balzac book which Pound himself had given her to read in their youth. This relation, which she calls the marriage of earth and heaven, indicates that coequal poets forge a hierogamic bond, where the characters are dynamic opposites, and thus form a balance of power. H.D. contrasts this bond, and its potential for equality, with the 'coordinated convention' for male–female relations, the one which is culturally secure: gender asymmetry.

> If the 'first love' is an uncoordinated entity, Angel-Devil – or Angel-Daemon or Daimon, Seraphitus–Seraphita – what then? Find a coordinated convention, Man-Hero who will compensate, complete the picture. (ETT, p. 19)

It has appeared to some critics as if H.D. simply shifted

from one convention to another; compensating for the loss of coequal love, by a rigid and guarded form of patriarchal sexuality: the idolising of an isolated, powerful father or lover.[21] A truer picture would see the positions of Daimon and Hero as the subjects of a major oscillation throughout her career, where she sought to create narrative and psychic strategies to regain the coequal bond of twinship between creative women and men. She attempts to organise the male figures in her life in ways to regain, in imagination, various stances empowering for women: freedom from romantic thraldom, or imaginative control of it, coequal twinship between men and women, female power directly experienced in repositioning 'the mother', and in debates with 'the father'. Her attempt to reorganise the male figure here gives Pound a multiplicity, from grey-haired inseminator of young disciples, to virile youth, to baby, golden-haired Eros. The stages of man move back and forth, rupturing the linear time of history and biography by psychological and mythic time, rupturing male power by imbedding it in interlocks of family relations.

These contradictory gender positions unite in *End to Torment*. First, she depicts herself and Pound as equals. Thus both H.D. and Pound have a 'confinement': Pound's is his years in St Elizabeth's, from which he is about to be released, and whose last imprisoned days form one of the ground bass recurrences, literalised and metaphorical, to which H.D. turns. H.D.'s confinement is her 'pregnancy' with this concept/conceptus of Pound, her labour with desire and the memory of desire, her sublimations of a piercing sexuality in ecstatic spiritual moments. In this work, as in 'Winter Love', she is inseminated by their 'fiery moment' (ETT, p.24). Her conceptus is by and of Pound, for she completes the autobiographical fiction with his rebirth from his imprisonment simultaneous with his birth from her confinement. But staggeringly – in a way typical of the erotics of these later works – her conceptus ends in the imaginary delivery of their imaginary child. She transposes the male figure down a generation now to exert a gender control where then she had felt herself overwhelmed by his power. The child who is typically born at these climactic moments in H.D.'s later works is another expression of a new age in gender relations: Eros in *End to Torment*, Espérance in 'Winter Love', Euphorion in *Helen in Egypt* all create a deliberate continuum between sexuality and spiritual transformation. The red-haired Eros, the brilliant red-haired pianists, Van Cliburn and Paderewski, the red-haired Pound are emanations of a unitary force of love. 'Desire begets love' because sexuality opens a spiritual reality.

The revisionary impulse of 'Winter Love' is consistent with *Helen in Egypt*. Here too we find that central figure in Western culture, the very image of the female with the destructive use of sexual desire, but voiceless, unjustified, heretofore unexamined. Like *Helen in Egypt* but more clearly here, H.D. argues that Helen has multiple identities, and she traces the paradox of her both causing and ending the Trojan War. Helen's sense of abandonment and betrayal in heterosexual love gives birth to the Helen 'that wrecked citadels'.[22] The Helen that could cause peace is the Helen of consummated maternal desire and homosexual nurturance.

'Winter Love's' 28 sections allude to the lunar (menstrual) cycle, and present Helen as the triple goddess of the moon.[23] She is the Artemisian or crescent maiden, sexually desirable but virginal; she is the Hecatean crone: a dark, swaddled figure in mourning for sexual betrayals and her sister/mother, the sage femme, who aids women in childbirth. Finally, she is the full maternal Helen, in bliss nursing her child.

There can be little doubt that 'Winter Love' was inspired by Pound's *Pisan Cantos*.[24] The atmosphere of intoxicating fruit, the references to apples and pomegranates allude to Pound's well-known 'Pomona' passage ('this fruit has a fire within it') which H.D. greatly admired. And the seduction of Helen by Odysseus occurs in a passage filled with references to a section of the Lynx Canto.[25] The sensual virile force and erotic natural smells ('the smell of pine mingles with rose leaves') are echoed directly by H.D., who evokes first the Dionysian presence of the lynx and then the fragrant, woody setting.

> Who has been here before?
> was it Iacchus, Dionysus, Bacchus?
> fragrance of grapes mingles with scent of cedar
>
> and apple-wood; though we have only fir-wood and
>   dried cones,
> alter-incense–and the hiss of resin . . .
>
> (WL. p.102)

The lovers are imagined in a hunting lodge; she is wrapped in a bunting of pelts. As in *Helen in Egypt*, here too the warmth and neo-maternal nurturance from a male figure allows memory to be activated. And this memory speaks itself as desire, results in insemination. Helen's most bliss-provoking consort is Song or Sun (Helios), no matter his particular form. At the same time she must mourn for the various widowhoods or betrayals that individual consorts provoke, she can re-enter these relationships through a new reality of the imagination, by poetic consummation. Further, the heterosexual moment of consummated desire, however lushly described, is not the resolution of the text, nor, finally, its emotional centre.

As well as insisting that bliss can come by the act of the poem, H.D. also insisted that heterosexual love is only completed by matrisexual passion – child to mother, mother to child. In that mother–child bond she includes the sororal services of love for both mother and child from another 'mother–child', a wise woman, clearly based on Bryher. Hence 'Winter Love' uses the experiential turning points of female identity (virginity, arousal, seduction, sexual consummation, childbirth, bliss of nursing), but especially focuses upon the intervention of a midwife, sage femme, who delivers Helen to motherhood. One may speak of the poem's ecstatic climaxes, two moments of erotic bliss: the climax in sexual honey, and the climax in maternal milk. If Odysseus's presence creates a sexual woman and the plot of romance, the sage femme's assistance creates matrisexuality, and pre-Oedipal erotics. A maternal Eros, based well within homosexual connections more than matches heterosexual Eros. All three balance structurally and emotionally: the closure of the poem is not singly the insemination of romance but also the 'golden bee' of the nursing child and the bond of Helen and her own midwife. Aphrodite contains both honey and milk.

'Hermetic Definition', H.D.'s last work, is based on the nine-month gestation period with its three trimesters. A thesis, antithesis and abrupt synthesis, it was begun in mid-August 1960 and completed in mid-February 1961.[26] She died in September 1961. The drama of authority centres here on a bold story of sexual desire not incidentally for a black man, a revelation of doubled possibilities for marginality and negotiation with Otherness to suggest a heterodox unification of those *en marge*.[27]

Rereading herself, H.D. treats the 1931 'Red Roses for Bronze', a poem transposing her attraction for Paul Robeson, as a prophecy of encounters with the Haitian journalist, Lionel Durand, and her emotional spurt of lust, energy, desire, pain. 'Hermetic Definition' intermingles citations from the early poem with text from Ambe(r)lain, the Freudian slip on his name (Amber- for Ambe-) had apparently come about to signal amber-eyed, dark-skinned Durand's connection, as Paris/Osiris/Bar-Isis, with the occult story chiselled into Notre Dame Cathedral, as Ambelain argues in a book quite familiar to H.D., *Dans l'ombre des cathédrales*.[28] The stones hold cultural secrets as H.D., an old woman, flares up with female secrets: an irrational, irrepressible desire and rush of sexual feeling, by which she feels imprisoned, which she herself calls excessive.

> Why did you come
> to trouble my decline?
> I am old (I was old till you came);
>
> the reddest rose unfolds,
> (which is ridiculous
> in this time, this place,
>
> unseemly, impossible,
> even slightly scandalous) . . .
>   (HD, p.3)

Yet of which she immediately says 'they've got to take that into account' (HD, p.3).

This mysterious *they* is not glossed, and yet is evidently those judges and critics of female writing and being to whom this poem responds both sexually and intellectually. The passion in 'Red Roses for Bronze' was still repressed in its energies, angry and jealous, and hence that poem of passion is rigidly pallid. Her newly-flaring rose in response to Durand's bronze is an insistence on

125

female erotic feeling as a valid source for poetic exploration. But to have come to that conclusion was no simple matter. Indeed, the first section of 'Hermetic Definition' discusses her own attempts to repress her sexual feelings because of her fears of judgement, her suspicion of this extraordinary fixation.

A male poet like Pound 'wouldn't hesitate' to speak of desire; but she (ironically) proposes the gender norm: 'perhaps humility is more becoming/in a woman' (HD, p.13). But her centred pride is coupled with a fierce need for approval: she therefore taxes her own style, her 'preciousness', a word in an unsigned review in *Newsweek* which she painfully though mistakenly thought Durand had written (HD, p.16).

How can a woman of an advanced age speak outright about a staggering – and virtually unreciprocated – sexual desire, and as well the 'unfaltering' desire to move towards a 'Lover'. How then to 'keep my identity' and enjoy as well the '*hachish supérieur*' of her sexual fantasy? (ibid., p.21). In short, how to have desire without romantic thraldom, although those interlocking scripts are culturally and psychologically annealed? These dilemmas occasion a pendulum swing into opposing claims.

The St-John Perse section, 'Groves of Academe', parses the words of a fellow poet whose imagination she, at every turn tests against her own, finding its scope, austerity, and distance from passion, provide 'formal and external' terms for transcendence of just this kind of erotic feeling (ibid., p.51). His imagery of a vast, 'unfathomable' geography, offers a model for poetry untroubled by spurts of uncontrollable passion (ibid., p.27). She admires to excess how his 'thought and range/ exceeds mine' (ibid., p.25). This St-John, like the character in *Jane Eyre*, offers spirit absolutely without erotics, or with a complete surpassing control; like the interplay between the polarised male characters in that novel, the intellectual thraldom is as damaging as the erotic.

Hence control of language is a metaphor for, or mate of, control of sexual feeling. In a letter to May Sarton, H.D. contrasted the 'pure silver' and the 'pure Attic' of the French language with the 'uncombed and bare-footed and altogether scrubby and with-moss-on-its knees' language she used as an American. Her longing for that elegant timbre made her then characterise her own work by a remarkable image of inferiority and otherness: 'we are just grubby children in the arts, patting our sand cakes to tin-moulds' whereas French poets (among whom Perse was to figure) 'are above us, beyond us'.[29] Further, their perfection is unconflictual; hers is filled with implicit, painful debate. 'Each perfected phrase, sea-shell, at ONE with thought-content – while our thoughts clash & sometimes *smash* our shells . . [H.D. ellipsis]. The poet shows in her consideration of Perse that some of the contrasts to which she had pointed in this letter on linguistic authority then still plagued her twenty-odd years later, but they have been reorganized by bold gender debates: French *vs.* American has become male transcendence *vs.* female immanence. And the female 'side' does not concede inferiority.

While St-John Perse's imaginative scope seems to pre-empt her interpretive and mythic space, H.D. locates their 'antithesis' or 'difference' (HD, pp. 30–1). 'I do not compete with your vast concept,/ the prick of pine-needles brings me back' (ibid., p.32). When she goes on to 'decipher' him, citing at length from several poems, she becomes more and more critical: 'But here, I don't know what you mean/ does anyone?' taxing him for words she doesn't 'understand anyway' (ibid., pp. 36, 43). His

H.D.

Perseus is 'perfection' but her gift, a 'small snake' (making allusion to even a minor Medusa head and snakes as female familiars) releases her to reconsider her 'humanity'. The physical handicap of old age, visible in her walk to the podium at the award ceremony of the American Academy of Arts and Letters ('is physical weakness indecent?', she asks), is memorialised with her emotional vulnerability to the sexual feelings 'Paris' (Durand) has evoked (HD, p.39). St-John Perse's steadying hand held to her is the gesture of a brother whom she judges and surpasses, for his vatic body/mind dualisms are exactly a block to erotic expression.

Thus by antithesis to Perse (though precisely aided from falling by him), she reclaims the experience of desire, refusing to enter into that patriarchal 'perfection' which his poetry represents. She returns to her poetry of particularity and need, with her small personal rituals (burning pine-cones) distinguishing herself from Perse's large horizons by informality, intimacy and vulnerability. But also, as is clearly stated in that letter to Robert Duncan, by a powerful sense of 'Risk'.

When she then finds Durand has died, in a great female *coup* of imagination, she takes the strange numerological clue (nine months between first meeting, and his death) as a sign and recasts her erotic obsession into imagined maternity: her 'Lover' becomes her child. The elegy, that familiar genre, has been mediated by gender, and becomes an annunciation, a pregnancy, a birth. Durand becomes alive not only in a transcendent way, typical of the elegy's setting of a new star in the sky; although Durand as 'Star of Day' is another version of the bronze, inseminating Helios who recurs in H.D.'s imaginative universe (HD, pp.45, 47). Durand is also re-animated as her child.

With broad biological allusions, H.D. follows the

course of pregnancy: 'you were five months "on the way"'; pensively alluding to abortion, with three months to go, 'it was too late to cast you out'; and finally: 'the cord is cut? no;/ I have nine months/to remember'; her 'emotional seizure' 'had to go on the full time [full term]'; 'the writing was the un-born,/ the conception' (ibid., pp.49, 52, 53, 54). Durand is memorialised as her baby and (in) her poem. The abrupt 'Now you are born/ and it's all over,/ will you leave me alone?' shows that this birth is also a kind of exorcism of a demanding incubus, in another unsentimental female statement. H.D.'s authority lies in her bold imaginative translation of her fixation. She has taken prime biological and sexual materials and broadcast them structurally and mythically. By the end of the poem, as she returns to post-partum singleness, the experience has led her to its immanent core: *the red rose/ the unalterable law . . ./ Night brings the Day* (ibid., p.55). As she said once, 'romance is resurrection in this life' (NRW, p. 58).

The Great Goddess Venus/Isis who stands behind this poem plays a special role at the beginning in liberating her from her shame. The Goddess, especially her intermingling of sexuality and maternality, of creation and procreation, of writing and Eros, is the commanding presence of maternal and erotic/ sexual authority who is created in many phases of H.D.'s *oeuvre*. Hence, she can stand as the necessary command for all the stages of exploration which this book has detailed.

> why must I write?
> you would not care for this,
> but She draws the veil aside,
>
> unbinds my eyes,
> commands,
> write, write or die.
>
> (HD, p.7)

As this study of H.D.'s career has indicated, to 'write, write or die', to follow this female command, is to traverse, repeatedly, the dilemmas which gender poses and to claim the authorities that one's gender offers for female creativity.

Notes

Preface

1. For example: Helene Moglen, *Charlotte Brontë: The Self Conceived* (W.W. Norton, New York, 1976); Jane Marcus's essays on Virginia Woolf, such as 'Thinking Back Through Our Mothers', in *New Feminist Essays on Virginia Woolf*, ed. Jane Marcus (University of Nebraska Press, Lincoln, 1981), pp. 1–30 and 'The Niece of a Nun: Virginia Woolf, Caroline Stephen, and the Cloistered Imagination', in *Virginia Woolf: A Feminist Slant*, ed. Jane Marcus (University of Nebraska Press, Lincoln, 1983), pp.7–36; Carolyn G. Heilbrun, 'Virginia Woolf in Her Fifties', in Marcus (ed.), *Feminist Slant*, pp.236–53. Susan Stanford Friedman's work on H.D., which will be alluded to a great deal here, is in this category as well.
2. Adrienne Rich, 'When We Dead Awaken: Writing as Re-Vision' (1971), in *On Lies, Secrets, and Silence: Selected Prose 1966–1978* (W.W. Norton, New York, 1979), p.43. Rich uses the more interpretive verb 'united', but that conceals an assumption about a correct, non-contradictory answer.
3. Myra Jehlen, 'Archimedes and the Paradox of Feminist Criticism', *Signs* 6, 4 (Summer 1981), pp.582–3. See also

131

Notes to pages xvi to 2

Lawrence Lipking, *The Life of the Poet: Beginning and Ending Poetic Careers* (University of Chicago Press, Chicago, 1981); he finds that the major turning point for a poetic career is learning 'to read one's early work, to explore its secret life and hidden meanings', p.15. This particular kind of re-reading occurred over the length of H.D.'s career; Jehlen's contribution, typical of a feminist understanding of women, is to see the interlock between needing to read oneself, and having to come to terms with others' reading of one in conventions of depiction. Jehlen: 'They [women and some non-hegemonic men] have to confront the assumptions that render them as a kind of fiction in themselves in that they are defined by others, as components of the language and thought of others', p.582.

4. Discussing issues of authority at all means a general indebtedness to Sandra Gilbert and Susan Gubar who summarised and pointed some of the parallel insights of contemporary writers like Adrienne Rich and Tillie Olsen. Their major question is how do women writers create strategies to forge female authority in the face of ideological prescriptions, and consequently anxiety, against such authority. *The Madwoman in the Attic: The Woman Writer and the Nineteenth-Century Literary Imagination* (Yale University Press, New Haven, 1979).

Chapter 1

1. Title phrase from H.D., *Palimpsest* (Southern Illinois University Press, Carbondale, 1968), p.130. Henceforward abbreviated P and cited in text. The novella, *Paint it To-day* (abbreviated PIT), source of the epigraph, is one of several of H.D.'s unpublished works of fiction from the 1920s. The Collection of American Literature, The Beinecke Rare Book and Manuscript Library, Yale University.

2. Elaine Showalter, 'Feminist Criticism in the Wilderness', *The New Feminist Criticism: Essays on Women, Literature and Theory*, ed. Elaine Showalter (Pantheon, New York, 1985); pp.243–70.

3. H.D., *Tribute to Freud* (1944, 1956 pub.) (David R. Godine,

Boston, 1974), p.38. Henceforth abbreviated TF and cited in text.

4. Sandra M. Gilbert and Susan Gubar, *The Madwoman in the Attic: The Woman Writer and the Nineteenth-Century Literary Imagination* (Yale University Press, New Haven, 1979), p.97.

5. Perdita Schaffner, 'The Egyptian Cat', in H.D., *Hedylus* (Black Swan Books, Redding Ridge, CT, 1980), p.145.

6. Nancy Miller, 'Emphasis Added: Plots and Plausibilities in Women's Fiction' (1981), in Showalter (ed.) (1985), pp. 339–60; Mary Jacobus, 'The Question of Language: Men of Maxims and *The Mill on the Floss*', *Writing and Sexual Difference*, ed. Elizabeth Abel (Chicago University Press, Chicago, 1982), pp.37–52; Rachel Blau DuPlessis, 'For the Etruscans' (1979), in Showalter (ed.) (1985), pp.271–91; Virginia Woolf, *Orlando* (New American Library, New York, first published 1928), p.204.

7. Especially in the first and second parts of her career, from 1912 to about 1933. Chapter 1 will treat the poetry through her *Collected Poems* (Liveright Publishing Corporation, New York, 1925); Chapter 2 will treat her early prose, especially the novels.

8. T.S. Eliot, 'Euripides and Professor Murray', *The Sacred Wood: Essays on Poetry and Criticism* (1920), (Methuen, London, 1960).

9. H.D., *Notes on Euripides, Pausanius, and Greek Lyric Poets*, 1918 (or earlier)–1920, Typescript, Beinecke Library, Yale University. Henceforward abbreviated in text as NEPG. H.D. also composed brisk, short reviews on classical scholarship for *Adelphi* (1925–27).

10. H.D. *Collected Poems, 1912–1944*, ed. Louis Martz (New Directions, New York, 1983), pp.412–13. Henceforward abbreviated in text as CP.

11. Suzanne Juhasz, *Naked and Fiery Forms: Modern American Poetry by Women: A New Tradition* (Harper and Row, New York, 1976), pp.1–3.

12. Alicia Ostriker, *Writing Like a Woman* (University of Michigan Press, Ann Arbor, 1983), p.1. See also *Stealing the Language*, Ostriker's book on American women's poetry, forthcoming from Beacon Press.

13. For biographical information, consult Susan Friedman, *Psyche Reborn: The Emergence of H.D.* (Indiana University

Press, Bloomington, 1981) and Friedman's major entry, 'H.D.', *Dictionary of Literary Biography: Modern American Poets* (Gale Research, Detroit, 1986); Barbara Guest, *Herself Defined: The Poet H.D. and Her World* (Doubleday, New York, 1984). As well, Vincent Quinn, *Hilda Doolittle* (Twayne, New York, 1967). To be used with some caution for its allegations and fixations on D.H. Lawrence, Janice Robinson, *H.D.: The Life and Work of an American Poet* (Houghton Mifflin, Boston, 1982).

14. H.D. to 'Billy'. Cited with the permission of The Poetry/ Rare Books Collection of the University Libraries, The State University of New York at Buffalo.

15. William Carlos Williams, *The Autobiography of William Carlos Williams* (Random House, New York, 1948), p.68.

16. Glenn Hughes, *Imagism and the Imagists* (Stanford University Press, Stanford, 1931), p.110.

17. Letter of H.D. to Norman Holmes Pearson, 12 March 1950, Beinecke Library.

18. Barbara Guest, who is quite interesting on the personal and literary exchanges by which H.D. made the transition from Pennsylvania to international poetry, is rightly concerned that Pound not be given the credit, but it is clear that H.D.'s repeated fictionalized presentation of her initiation into a poetic career emphasised Pound. See Guest, p.5.

19. H.D., *End to Torment* (1958), (New Directions, New York, 1979), p.18. Henceforward abbreviated as ETT.

20. Both Susan Friedman and Adalaide Morris, in forthcoming book-length studies of, respectively, H.D.'s 'sagas of the self' in her prose and H.D.'s special thematic vocabulary, her 'lexicon', promise to consider the topic of H.D.'s pseudonyms.

21. Margaret Homans, *Women Writers and Poetic Identity: Dorothy Wordsworth, Emily Brontë and Emily Dickinson* (Princeton University Press, Princeton, 1980), p. 3.

22. Marianne DeKoven, *A Different Language: Gertrude Stein's Experimental Writing* (The University of Wisconsin Press, Madison, 1983), p. xviii.

23. Jeanne Kammer, 'The Art of Silence and the Forms of Women's Poetry', *Shakespeare's Sisters: Feminist Essays on Women Poets*, ed. Sandra M. Gilbert and Susan Gubar (Indiana University Press, Bloomington, 1979), pp.153–64.

24. Richard Aldington (trans.), *The Poems of Anyte of Tegea* (The Egoist Ltd, London, 1919, in The Poets' Translation Series). The sequence of influence (H.D. to Aldington or vice versa) cannot be clear from dates of publication.
25. Letter, Richard Aldington to H.D., 3 January 1919, Beinecke Library. Ezra Pound also noted, in 1917, that H.D. had 'spoiled the "few but perfect" position which she might have held to'–one might in retrospect see this as the perfect script for a poetess: 'utterly narrow minded she-bard'. *The Letters of Ezra Pound: 1907–1941*, ed. D.D. Paige (Harcourt, Brace & World, New York, 1950), pp. 114, 157.
26. Cyrena N. Pondrom, 'H.D. and the Origins of Imagism', *Sagetrieb* 4, 1 (1985), pp.73–97.
27. Ezra Pound, *Poetry* I (November 1912), p. 65, cited in Quinn, p. 21.
28. Ezra Pound, 'Vorticism', *Gaudier-Brzeska: A Memoir* (1916) (New Directions, New York, 1970), p. 89.
29. Adalaide Morris, 'The Concept of Projection: H.D.'s Visionary Powers', *Contemporary Literature* 25, 4 (Winter 1984), p. 416. See the section, so titled in Mina Loy, *The Last Lunar Baedeker*, Roger L. Conover (ed.) (The Jargon Society, Highlands, N.C., 1982), pp.267–86, including 'Feminist Manifesto'.
30. Certain discussions of poetry in the novel *Hedylus* sound like reweavings of 'Some Don't for Imagists', but in this context H.D. de-emphasises the 'radical' nature of imagism, embarking instead on a classicising effort to justify imagism because it recovered the poetic principles of antiquity.
31. Susan Stanford Friedman, 'Palimpsests of Origin in H.D.'s Career', forthcoming, *Poesis*.
32. This dilemma is studied in Susan Gubar, '"The Blank Page" and the Issues of Female Creativity', Showalter (ed.) (1985), pp. 292–313.
33. 'A Note on Poetry', *Oxford Anthology of American Literature*, ed. William Rose Benét and Norman Holmes Pearson (Oxford University Press, New York, 1938), p. 1288.
34. Nancy J. Vickers, 'Diana Described: Scattered Woman and Scattered Rhyme', Abel (ed.) (1983), pp. 95–109. The citation, from Laura Mulvey, 'Visual Pleasure and Narrative Cinema', *Screen* 16 (1975), cited in Vickers, p. 109.

35. Julia Kristeva, *Desire in Language: A Semiotic Approach to Literature and Art* (Columbia University Press, New York, 1980), p. 69.
36. Norman Holmes Pearson, 'An Interview on H.D.' with L.S. Dembo, *Contemporary Literature: Special Issue on H.D.*, 10, 4 (Autumn 1969), pp. 435–46.
37. There are still poems in which the 'I' yearns to merge into a 'you'–'Evadne', 'Leda', 'Circe'.
38. The analysis that H.D. educated herself in the three major genres of Greek writing draws out what is implied in Swann. In his study of the classical elements in H.D., Swann sees her as merely 'a belated *Anthology* poet' with the further implication that she pursued the Greeks to an excessive degree. Thomas Burnett Swann, *The Classical World of H.D.* (University of Nebraska Press, Lincoln, 1963), p. 73.
39. H.D., *Notes on Thought and Vision* (1919), including 'The Wise Sappho', a chapter from NEPG (City Lights Books, San Francisco, 1982), p. 32. Henceforward cited in text as NTV.
40. H.D., *Bid Me to Live (A Madrigal)* (1939/1949/1960 pub.) (Black Swan Books, Redding Ridge, CT, 1983), p. 163. Henceforward abbreviated BMTL. Also published by Virago.
41. See *The Poems of Meleager*, trans. Peter Whigham, Introduction and literal translations by Peter Jay (University of California Press, Berkeley, 1975). Richard Aldington published a translation of Meleager of Gadara in his *Medallions in Clay* (Alfred Knopf, New York, 1921).
42. The poems are Meleagrian because they contain imbeddings translated from his work while setting his words in her dramatic context. *Palatine Anthology* 5, 144, 147.
43. Meryl Altman's paper 'On Knowing Greek: H.D.'s Literary History' (unpublished) also has a significant reading of 'Heliodora', showing how the poem – between brother poets – is completed by the daring of the female writer – H.D. herself. Altman reflects on a stance which she argues is paradigmatic for H.D.'s career as a whole: 'The act of writing, which initially produced confusion and anxiety about gender role, identity, and ability, itself provides the means for surmounting that confusion' (Ts. pp. 23–4). Altman and I have come independently to

similar conclusions about the engendering of Greece in H.D.'s career.

44. Indeed, alas, even necessary words are missing. Hugh Kenner's admirable argument but outrageously incomplete literary history in *The Pound Era* (University of California Press, Berkeley, 1971) notably claims Sappho for male modernists Pound and Aldington while completely neglecting H.D.'s contributions to both the enterprises of Imagism and cross-temporal collaboration.

45. Susan Gubar, 'Sapphistries' *Signs* 10, 1 (Autumn 1984), pp. 43–62. Gubar discusses the concept of 'contemporary collaboration' linking writers to a past they must fabricate, and shows Sappho's role as a special precursor to lesbian writers like Renée Vivian and to H.D.

46. Louis Martz, 'Introduction', *Collected Poems of H.D.*, pp. xiv–xviii.

47. Alicia Ostriker, citing Claudine Herrmann. ' "Thieves of Language": Women Poets and Revisionist Mythmaking' (1982), Showalter (ed.) (1985), pp. 314–38. This citation from Ostriker, 'Comment on Homans', *Signs* 10, 3 (Spring 1985), p. 600.

48. Friedman on 'Callypso [sic] Speaks' and 'Helen', Ostriker on 'Demeter' and DuPlessis on 'Eurydice' should all be consulted, respectively in *Psyche Reborn*, pp. 232–43, *Writing Like a Women*, pp. 24–5, and *Writing Beyond the Ending: Narrative Strategies of Twentieth-Century Women Writers* (Indiana University Press, Bloomington, 1985), pp. 70–1, 105–10.

49. Richard Aldington, 'Lesbia', *Collected Poems* (Covici, Friede Publishers, New York, 1928), p. 10.

Chapter 2

1. Through the 1920s and up to the year (1960) before her death, consisting of novels which are often *romans à clef*, and autobiographical essay-memoirs. Not all of these have been published, not all those published are equally accessible. H.D. also wrote historical-mystical novels in the 1940s and 1950s like *The Sword Went Out to Sea, White Rose and the Red*, and *The Mystery*. The majority of the unpublished materials are deserving of publication and

critical notice. For this overview, I concentrate on the published and accessible texts.

2. H.D. used the term 'Madrigal cycle' in *Thorn Thicket* (1960), Beinecke Library, p. 28. I've volunteered the other terms. This work abbreviated TT.

3. Letter, 4 July 1918, Beinecke Library, cited by Susan Friedman in 'Ghost Stories: H.D.'s *Hedylus*', *Sagetrieb* 4, 2/3 (Fall & Winter 1985), pp. 325–33.

4. 29 March 1927 or 1928, to Viola Jordan, Beinecke Library, cited in Susan Friedman, *Psyche Reborn*, p. 6.

5. Dorothy Dinnerstein, *The Mermaid and the Minotaur: Sexual Arrangements and Human Malaise* (Harper and Row, Publishers, New York, 1976); Simone de Beauvoir, *The Second Sex* (1949), trans. H.M. Parshley (Bantam Books, New York, 1961).

6. Luce Irigaray, *This Sex Which is Not One* (1977), trans. Catherine Porter with Carolyn Burke (Cornell University Press, Ithaca, 1985), p. 81. Jonathan Culler also sees the acts of minimising difference and maximising difference as related fronts of feminist criticism. *On Deconstruction: Theory and Criticism after Structuralism* (Cornell University Press, Ithaca, 1982).

7. Virginia Woolf, *A Room of One's Own* (1929) (Harcourt, Brace and World, 1957), p. 88. Henceforward abbreviated AROO.

8. Adrienne Rich, 'Compulsory Heterosexuality and Lesbian Existence', *Signs* 5, 4 (Summer 1980), pp. 631–60.

9. Carolyn Burke, 'Introduction to Luce Irigaray's "When Our Lips Speak Together" ', *Signs* 6, 1 (Autumn 1980), p. 67; Irigaray, *Speculum*, 'Notes on Selected Terms', p. 222.

10. Adalaide Morris, 'Reading H.D.'s "Helios and Athene" ', *The Iowa Review*, 12, 2 (Spring/Summer 1981), pp. 155–63. This succinct introduction sets this text in relation to later writing by H.D.

11. Useful and provocative ideas about H.D.'s relationship with D.H. Lawrence come in Sandra Gilbert's review of recent H.D. scholarship, with emphasis on the book by Janice Robinson. 'H.D.? Who Was She?', *Contemporary Literature* 24, 4 (Winter 1983), pp. 496–511.

12. Susan Gubar, 'The Birth of the Artist as Heroine: (Re)production, the *Kunstlerroman* Tradition, and the Fiction of Katharine Mansfield', in *The Representation of*

Women in Fiction, ed. Carolyn G. Heilbrun and Margaret R. Higonnet (The Johns Hopkins University Press, Baltimore, 1983), pp. 19–59; Rachel Blau DuPlessis, 'To "bear my mother's name": *Kunstlerromane* by Women Writers', in *Writing Beyond the Ending*; Bell Gale Chevigny, 'Daughters Writing: Toward a Theory of Women's Biography', in *Between Women*, ed. Carol Ascher, Louise DeSalvo, Sara Ruddick (Beacon Press, Boston, 1984), pp. 357–79; Hélène Cixous, 'The Laugh of the Medusa', in *New French Feminisms*, ed. Elaine Marks and Isabelle de Courtivron (The University of Massachusetts Press, Amherst, 1980), pp. 245–64.

13. Hedylus is an historical poet and was also mentioned by Meleager; both Hedylus' mother Hedyle and his grandmother Moschine were historically attested poets, information which H.D. does not use. H.D., *Hedylus* (1928) (Black Swan Books, Redding Ridge, CT, 1980); further references in text as H.

14. H.D., *Notes on Recent Writing* (1949), Beinecke Library, pp. 74, 9/10. Henceforward cited in text as NRW.

15. Incidentally, these lines rewrite and re-pose the elegy for Corinth by the real male poet, Antipater of Sidon. He also wrote the epigram to Hipparchia, our character's mother. By this use of actual and fictional materials woven together, H.D. continues the tradition she revises, revises the tradition she continues.

16. Deborah Kelly Kloepfer, 'Flesh Made Word: Maternal Inscription in H.D.', *Sagetrieb* 3, 1 (Spring 1984), pp. 27–48. Citation, p. 34.

17. Virginia Woolf, 'Women and Fiction', in *Granite and Rainbow* (Harcourt Brace and Company, New York, 1958), p. 81; AROO, p. 96.

18. Although Perdita Schaffner confirmed with Susan Friedman that H.D. 'owned many, if not all, of Woolf's books and read them avidly' (Friedman, *Psyche Reborn*, p. 305), H.D.'s remarks on Woolf seem to be limited to excited thanks for the loan of a book, possibly *A Room of One's Own* (letter to Brigit Patmore, cited by Friedman), and some pensive comments on Woolf's suicide in letters (e.g. to Mary Herr, at Bryn Mawr College, to May Sarton in The Berg Collection, New York Public Library) and in an as yet unpublished short story.

19. It is important to emphasise that female gender does not privilege access to that voice/stance in language; indeed, female gender issues may set up particular impediments to semiotic exploration. For example, in poetic production, the congruence between female gender identity and a research into the 'chora' evokes psychic dangers (merging, lack of separation, inability to distance from the production) while in poetic reception, a woman 'entering' that position may be more taxed with artlessness, mimesis of the female mushy mind, confession/expression of what they (we) cannot help being, and so forth.

20. The allusion is to the opening sentence of the prose part of H.D.'s *By Avon River* (Macmillan, New York, 1949). Evelyn Haller suggests that Egypt offered women writers an alternative to what was perceived as masculinist Graeco-Roman myths. 'Isis Unveiled: Virginia Woolf's Use of Egyptian Myth', in *Virginia Woolf: A Feminist Slant*, ed. Jane Marcus (University of Nebraska Press, Lincoln, 1983), pp. 109–31.

21. *Pilate's Wife* (1924), Beinecke Library, p. 25.

22. The Borderline group includes 'Narthex' (1931), *The Usual Star* and *Two Americans* (Imprimerie Darantière, Dijon, 1934), *Kora and Ka* and *Mira Mare* (Imprimerie Darantière, Dijon, 1934), *Nights* (Imprimerie Darantière, Dijon, 1935), 'Pontikonisi (Mouse Island)' *Pagany* III, 3 (July–September 1932), pp. 1–9, under the pseudonym Rhoda Peter. The novellas were privately printed.

23. Current work on H.D. and cinema includes Anne Friedberg's reconstruction of some of *Wing Beat* (1927) and *Foothills* (1929), two POOL group films, now at the Museum of Modern Art. See also Anne Friedberg, 'Approaching *Borderline*', *Millenium Film Journal*, nos 7–9 (Fall–Winter 1980–81), pp. 130–9; Friedberg, ' "All the light within the light fascinates me.": Fragments from the Film *Wing Beat* – H.D.'s Film Work in Context', Modern Language Association Special Session 437, 1980; Charlotte Mandel, 'Magical Lenses: Poet's Vision Beyond the Naked Eye', forthcoming in *H.D., Woman and Poet*, ed. Michael King (National Poetry Foundation, Orono, Maine, 1986); Mandel, 'Garbo/Helen: The Self-Projection of Beauty by H.D.', *Women's Studies* 7, nos 2–3 (1980), pp. 127–35. Also see Morris (1984), especially the section on cinematic

projection. A remarkable consideration of H.D. and photographic images occurs in Diana Collecutt, 'Images at the Crossroads: The "H.D. Scrapbook" ', in the King anthology.

24. The three articles of the meditation 'The Cinema and the Classics' are, respectively, in the three first issues of *Close Up* I, 1 (July 1927), pp. 22–33; I, 2 (August 1927), pp. 30–9; and I, 3 (November 1927), pp. 18–31.

25. 'Narthex', *The [Second] American Caravan: A Yearbook of American Literature*, ed. Alfred Kreymborg, Lewis Mumford and Paul Rosenfeld (Macaulay, New York, 1928), pp. 225–84. Citation from p. 273.

26. Novels of the Madrigal cycle are: *Paint it To-day* (1921), *Asphodel* (1921–22), which remain unpublished; *Her* (1927), pubished as *HERmione*, and *Bid Me to Live (A Madrigal)* (1960).

27. Susan Friedman and Rachel Blau DuPlessis, ' "I Had Two Loves Separate": The Sexualities of H.D.'s *Her*', discuss the public muting of lesbian bonds and the concentration on plots of romantic thraldom. *Montemora* 8 (1981), pp. 3–30.

28. H.D., *HERmione* (1927) (New Directions, New York, 1981). Henceforward abbreviated HER.

29. John Berger, *Ways of Seeing* (Penguin Books, London, 1972), p. 46.

30. Virginia Woolf, *To the Lighthouse* (1927) (Harcourt, Brace and World, New York, 1955), p. 79.

31. Catharine Stimpson, 'Zero Degree Deviancy: The Lesbian Novel in English', in *Writing and Sexual Difference*, ed. Abel, pp. 243–59.

Chapter 3

1. Source of chapter title is *Tribute to Freud*, p. 99; source of epigraph is 'The Master', CP, p. 455.

2. H.D., 'Conrad Veidt', *Close Up* I, 3 (September 1927), p. 42.

3. *Advent*, worked on in 1933, assembled in 1948, first published in 1956, both opens and closes this period (1933–48) of H.D.'s writing. Included are *The Gift*, composed 1941–43, partially published 1982; *Trilogy*, written 1942–44, published 1944 and 1946; and *Writing on*

the Wall ('assembled', as she says [NRW, p. 26] in 1944), which is the main part of *Tribute to Freud*. As well there is a portrait of Freud in *Helen in Egypt* and the address to Freud in the poem called 'The Master'. Tracing out the subtle differences in H.D.'s various discussions of Freud in poems published and unpublished, memoirs, and correspondence, for her forthcoming study of the letters about H.D.'s analysis, Susan Friedman reports that 'the more private the genre, the more suitable the form for an exploration of gender'. Typescript, 'Introduction', *Portrait of an Analysis with Freud: The H.D.–Bryher Letters, 1933–34*, p. 18.

4. H.D. letter to Robert McAlmon, 18 August 193[5], Beinecke Library.

5. Robert Duncan is particularly eloquent on the Shelleyean imperative: modernist poets 'stand at the beginning of a phase in poetry that has not ended. . . . Their threshold remains ours. The time of war and exploitation, the infamy and lies of the new capitalist war-state, continue. And the answering intensity of the imagination to hold its own values must continue'. 'Rites of Participation' [*H.D. Book*, Part I, Ch. 6] in *A Caterpillar Anthology*, ed. Clayton Eshleman (Doubleday, New York, 1971), p. 53.

6. *Asphodel*, Part II, p. 3. Beinecke Library.

7. *The Gift*, Typescript, Ch. IV, 'Because One is Happy', pp. 1–2, Beinecke Library.

8. H.D. letter to Marianne Moore, 27 June [1940]. Rosenbach Museum and Library.

9. H.D. letter to Robert McAlmon, 18 August 193[5]. Beinecke Library.

10. I am borrowing Sandra Gilbert's summary of Susan Friedman's work: 'H.D.'s struggle to be educated by Freud without being indoctrinated by him is symbolic of every women artist's struggle to assimilate the wisdom of Western civilisation without acquiescing in its misogyny'. 'H.D. Who Was She?', *Contemporary Literature* 24, 4 (Winter 1983), p. 506.

11. Hayden V. White, 'Foucault Decoded: Notes from Underground', *History and Theory* 12, 1 (1973), pp. 41–2.

12. The very fact that H.D. sought psychoanalysis has been interpreted curiously by such early critics as Riddel who, in Marylin Arthur's reading, reenact the Freudian master

plot, 'in which the male/critic/analyst hears the voice of the female/poet/patient as a lamentation over loss, incompleteness, subjectivity, and insubstantiality'. 'Psycho-Mythology: The Case of H.D.', *Bucknell Review* 28, 2 (1983), p. 66.

13. *The Gift* (New Directions, New York, 1982), to be abbreviated G in text, lamentably is not faithful to H.D.'s finished manuscript; editorial work on the manuscript is veiled, without explanatory note, guidelines, or principles. Central passages–lyrical reflection and meditation, images and thematic materials which are motific and recur, Moravian wisdom tales, shifts into another dimension, descriptions of being a civilian under World War II bombs, descriptions of the practice of visualisation–are cut without justification or warning. (Thanks to Diana Collecott, warning is given to the editorial abridgements in the publication of *The Gift* by Virago: see *TLS*, 15 February 1985, p. 171.) Chapter epigraphs are gone. Capitalisation is sometimes normalised, sometimes not. Section markers are sometimes suppressed. H.D.'s own interesting notes are unpublished. Even a whole chapter (Ch. 2) disappeared. See Bibliography for sources of accurately published chapters.

14. Thus in many particulars (maternal inspiration, large 'Victorian' family, intellectual father, early childhood sexual abuse), this memoir could be compared to Virginia Woolf's *Moments of Being*.

15. Barbara Guest's useful findings put the literal event into perspective, *Herself Defined*, pp. 18–19.

16. Claire Buck, 'Freud and H.D.–bisexuality and a feminine discourse', *M/F* 8 (1983), pp. 61, 63.

17. *The Gift*, Typescript, Ch. V, 'The Secret', p. 40.

18. While in the earlier works, H.D. seems to console herself with being one of an élite vanguard of heterodox seekers/ seers (as in the early lyric, 'Cities', CP, pp. 39–42), in the post-World War II work, despite arcana, her political vision became more democratic, and she felt that all must do–and were capable of doing–important spiritual work on themselves which would bring about an accretive social change, building cell by cell, like coral or honeycomb.

19. This is Adalaide Morris's point, in her study of *Tribute to*

Freud in the forthcoming *H.D.'s Lexicon*.

20. 'Perfect bi—' from H.D. letter to Bryher, 24 November 1934. Beinecke Library.

21. Kristeva, *Desire in Language*, pp. 133–40.

22. Theodor Adorno, 'The Essay as Form', trans. Bob Hullot-Kenter and Frederic Will, *New German Critique* 32 (Spring–Summer 1984), pp. 159–66.

23. In a major meditation on modernism, the impact of *Trilogy* and H.D., Robert Duncan reminds us repeatedly that 'men live uneasily with or under the threat of genius in women', later naming this, after *Trilogy* III, 'the Simon complex – a religious orthodoxy and a literary orthodoxy in a guise of criticism that must *"draw the line somewhere"* to exclude the female revelation'. Duncan [*The H.D. Book*, II, Ch. 9], *Chicago Review* 30, 3 (Winter 1979), pp. 43, 68–9.

24. In his introduction, Pearson cites from a letter to him: 'I really DID feel that a new heaven and a new earth were about to materialise.' H.D. to Norman Holmes Pearson, December 1944, cited in the 1973 New Directions edition of *Trilogy*, p. ix.

25. Friedman first indicated in *Psyche Reborn*, pp. 74–6, that the whole poem was inspired by the 'tripod' and its triple scientia; this reading will extend her insight to the structures of argument.

26. *Oxford Anthology of American Literature*, p. 1287.

27. Susan Gubar, 'The Echoing Spell of H.D.'s *Trilogy*', in *Shakespeare's Sisters*, ed. Gilbert and Gubar, p. 202.

28. DuPlessis, *Writing Beyond the Ending*, pp. 116–21.

29. See also Friedman's explanation that this language was influenced by Freud's ideas about the linguistic evidence left by the unconscious. *Psyche Reborn*, pp. 51–5.

30. Point made by Karen Fasano, undergraduate student at Temple University, Spring 1984.

31. See Susan Gubar, ' "The Blank Page" and the Issue of Female Creativity', in Showalter (ed.) (1985).

32. On John as source and the importance of a revisionary look at Revelations, see Norman Holmes Pearson's 'Foreword' in the 1973 New Directions *Trilogy* which cites a number of letters from H.D. on her sources; see Friedman, who traces the allusions to Revelations and discusses at length John's place in a misogynist tradition which misapprehends the fertility goddesses (*Psyche*

Reborn, pp. 246–53); see Gubar, who also shows how H.D. makes a critique of John's vengeful and presumptive stance ('The Echoing Spell', *Shakespeare's Sisters*, pp. 209–11).

33. These notes were first published in *Montemora* 8 (1981); see Bibliography, primary sources.
34. *The Listener* 57 (9 May 1957), p. 753.
35. 'Sagesse' in *Hermetic Definition* (New Directions, New York, 1972), p. 66.

Chapter 4

1. The chapter title is from the poem 'Priest' from the collection, deliberately unpublished by H.D., called *A Dead Priestess Speaks* (CP, 423). This collection served as a source-book for *Trilogy* and *Helen in Egypt*. In context, the poem continues a dialogue with a long past, but recently refound 'lover', who, importantly, was the subject of one of H.D.'s hallucinatory experiences of the 1920s. In the poem, she compares sexual desire to platinum, radium or any white luminosity, and makes sure her imaginary auditor knows that consummated desire is not of interest. 'Desire begets/ love' is her precise, bold, and in this context, somewhat contemptuous explanation: personal experiences of passion have a transcendent function, leading to spiritual revelation. In effect she announces to Rodeck, a newly-ordained Episcopal priest, that her heterodox spiritual passion is superior to his orthodoxy.
2. Virginia Woolf, 'Professions for Women', *Collected Essays*, *Vol. II* (Harcourt, Brace and World, New York), 1967, p. 44.
3. See 'Romantic Thralldom and "Subtle Genealogies" in H.D.', in *Writing Beyond the Ending*, pp. 66–83.
4. Letter to Sylvia Dobson, 31 May 1934; 'A Friendship Traced', ed. Carol Tinker, *Conjunctions* 2 (1982), p. 119.
5. Not coincidentally, H.D. was hailed by friends as a new Garbo for her work in *Borderline*.
6. 'The Mask the the Movietone' (The Cinema and the Classics III), *Close Up* I (November 1927), p. 19; 'Beauty' (The Cinema and The Classics I), *Close Up* I (July 1927), pp. 25, 27.

7. 'The Mask and the Movietone', *Close Up* I (November 1927), p. 31.

8. The earliest Helen by H.D. was a commentary on Euripides' play, 'Helen in Egypt', NEPG. It is distinguished by intense visualisations of setting, character, gesture, garment, natural sign. Already, H.D.'s revisionary and critical reading is taking shape. 'It is good to meet Helen face to face, for men and poets have visualised her so crudely. We had come to cloy with her sweetness, her contours painted for us, as soft and luxurious' ('Helen in Egypt', in NEPG, Part I, p. 3). This is in keeping with a far later remark, in a letter of 31 January 1956, to Norman Holmes Pearson. 'I felt quite ill – [she says of a film]. They always make H[elen] of T[roy] a cutie – is it the male conception? she was a Spartan, a goddess, etc. Well – I suppose mere-man cannot swallow that.' Beinecke Library.

9. As I begin the reading of this difficult poem, it is important to note the continued pall which the 'double critical standard' (in Elaine Showalter's phrase) exerts on the work of women, for this major long poem, like *Trilogy*, is virtually unread while long poems by Eliot, Stevens, Pound, and Williams have been subjected to extensive and rewarding critical scrutiny, a scrutiny that itself has effectively proposed a modernism to new generations of readers and critics.

10. H.D., *Helen in Egypt*, (New Directions, New York, 1961), p. 13. Title is subsequently abbreviated HE.

11. Teresa de Lauretis, *Alice Doesn't: Feminism, Semiotics, Cinema* (Indiana University Press, Bloomington, 1984), pp. 25–9.

12. The myth demands revision, for its misuse is punishing. H.D. evokes Stesichorus, author of an anti-Helen ode, who was thereupon punished by a blin⌐ ⌐s not revoked until he retracted and re-saw his former story.

13. Carolyn Burke, 'Supposed Persons: Modernist Poetry and the Female Subject (a Review Essay)', *Feminist Studies* 11, 1 (Spring 1985), pp. 131–48.

14. In a section of *H.D.'s Lexicon* (forthcoming, Indiana University Press), Adalaide Morris argues that H.D.'s poem 'disturbs and disperses' the genre of the epic by attention to the ideologies (hierarchy, contentiousness, conquest) that lie at its root.

15. Alice Jardine, 'Pre-Texts for the Transatlantic Feminist', *Yale French Studies* 62 (1981), p. 221, herself paraphrasing Jean-Joseph Goux, *Economie et symbolique* and *Les Iconoclastes* (Paris, Editions du Seuil, respectively 1973 and 1978) and suggesting a trope not unfamiliar in the recurrent, golden age critique of Western civilisation.

16. The works in question are *Notes on Recent Writing* (1949), literary and autobiographical essay; *Magic Mirror* (1955), autobiographical novel; *Compassionate Friendship* (1955), memoir; *Hirslanden Notebooks* (1957–59), daybook or journal; *Vale Ave* (1957), long poem; *End to Torment* (1958/1979 pub.), memoir; *Thorn Thicket* (1960), journal/memoir; as well as two of the poems published in *Hermetic Definition* (pub. 1972): 'Winter Love' (1959) and 'Hermetic Definition' (1960–61). All the unpublished work is housed at Beinecke Library. Henceforth *Compassionate Friendship* will be abbreviated CF.

17. Precisely the range and array of 'brother-lovers' are vital to H.D.'s personal legend. Thus while a critic might argue that she was fixated on each and all, it would be impossible to hold that H.D. was fixated on only one, as Janice Robinson does. For a devastating, factual answer to Robinson, see also Susan Friedman, ' "Remembering Shakespeare always, but remembering him differently": H.D.'s *By Avon River*', *Sagetrieb* 2, 2 (Summer–Fall 1983), p. 50.

18. As H.D. said in *Advent*, her recurrent attempts to write and to use her hallucinatory experiences were a refusal to give them up, to reduce them, repress or forget them. This is her stubbornness, crucial emotional underpinning to the claim of female authority, and for it she uses the metaphor of Penelope's work: 'It is obviously Penelope's web that I am weaving' (TF, 153).

19. Written originally for different communities, both Robert Duncan's *H.D. Book* and Susan Friedman's *Psyche Reborn* link H.D.'s work to sources in occult and hermetic tradition.

20. Michel Foucault, *The History of Sexuality, Volume 1: An Introduction* (1976), trans. Robert Hurley (Vintage Books, New York, 1980).

21. For example, Paul Smith's comment in the chapter on H.D. in *Pound Revised* (Croom Helm, London, 1983). After

an elegant exposition of the way Helen 'stands for another kind of writing presided over by the images of weaving and enigmatic script' which is a deliberate answer to patriarchal activities of writing, Smith says 'The deficiency, as I see it, of H.D.'s work lies in its ultimate resolution of this new separateness, the multiple hieroglyphs of the woven thread, into the word of an all-powerful godfather'. Smith takes Amen, in Part I of *Trilogy* and early in *Helen in Egypt*, as a 'ratificatory signature to [the whole] text, as the amen of imprecation or of the profession of faith' and says that 'Amen dissipates some of the force of H.D.'s enquiry' which Smith takes to be, very interestingly, the creation of a metonymic writing of complete female difference (p. 125). There is no doubt that this is crucial, and Smith's is an excellent reading, but he does not see the desire to renegotiate with male presence as anything but capitulation. One could see it ideologically as a desire to forge a new compact between the sexes; stylistically, as the desire to rebalance semiotic and symbolic modes.

22. 'Winter Love' to be abbreviated WL, and 'Hermetic Definition' or HD are both published with 'Sagesse' in *Hermetic Definition* (New Directions, New York, 1972). The citation is from HD, p. 92.

23. H.D. knew Robert Graves' *The White Goddess* and took notes on it in her *Helen in Egypt* composition notebooks (Friedman, *Psyche Reborn*, p. 269).

24. H.D. maintained an interesting correspondence with both Ezra Pound and Richard Aldington in the last years of her life.

25. See ETT, p. 34; Ezra Pound, *The Pisan Cantos* in *The Cantos of Ezra Pound* (New Directions, New York, 1948), pp. 68, 67.

26. While the large inspiration was Durand, the specific incitement to write the poem came in correspondence with Robert Duncan, to whom she said, in a letter of 6 September [1960]: 'I just *wasn't* going to write any poetry & then your letter came & the poem, & Aug. 17, it started me off. Does one *have* to write? It seems so, from your *Risk*. Mine is a Risk, too.' From the context, the 'Risk' is clearly the naming of erotic passion. Beinecke Library.

27. Susan Stanford Friedman, 'The Modernism of the "Scattered Remnant": Race and Politics in H.D.'s Development' argues that 'H.D.'s personal experiences with

the issue of racism in the late twenties and early thirties
[in her bond with Paul Robeson] played a key role in
deepening and broadening her early feminism into a fully
progressive modernism based on an identification with all
the people who exist as "the scattered remnant" at the
fringes of culture' (Ts., p. 2; forthcoming in *H.D.: Woman
and Poet*, ed. Michael King).
28. For a useful exposition of the allusions in the poem, see
Vincent Quinn, especially the tie between Paris (the city),
Notre Dame (the cathedral), and an old temple of Isis
alleged to have stood on that very spot in Paris. 'H.D.'s
"Hermetic Definition": The Poet as Archetypal Mother',
Contemporary Literature 18, 1 (Winter 1977), pp. 51–61.
29. Letter to May Sarton, 17 August [1939], Henry W. and
Albert A. Berg Collection, The New York Public Library,
Astor, Lenox and Tilden Foundations.

Selected Bibliography

Primary Texts

The dating of H.D.'s works is much more complicated than the dating of an equivalent writer, such as Virginia Woolf, whose publication normally followed upon composition. First, some important novels and memoirs are, as yet, unpublished. Second, H.D. composed some of her works over several interrupted periods; the publication date of *Bid Me To Live* hardly reflects its realities of composition, yet composition dates must be accounted for in a critical study. H.D. dated her final works, and she offered chronological/thematic readings in some of her autobiographical memoirs. This list contains both published and unpublished works in an approximate order of composition. In dating H.D., I have depended heavily upon and drawn upon a chronological chart of H.D.'s works, including years of composition and year(s) of publication, prepared by Susan Stanford Friedman. I would like to record my gratitude to her for making this chart available to me.

For more detailed information, accurate to 1969, and including periodical publication of both poetry and prose, as well as a list of works about H.D., see 'H.D.: A

Preliminary Checklist' drawn up by Jackson R. Bryer and Pamela Roblyer, *Contemporary Literature* 10, 4 (Autumn 1969), pp.632-75.

Sea Garden. Boston, Houghton Mifflin, 1916. Now in CP.
Choruses from Iphigenia at Aulis. London, The Egoist Press, 1916. Now in CP.
Choruses from the Iphigenia in Aulis and the Hippolytus of Euripides. The Poet's Translation Series. London, The Egoist Limited, 1919. Now in CP.
Notes on Thought and Vision. (1919) San Francisco, City Lights Books, 1982. (Abbreviated NTV.)
Hymen. London, The Egoist Press, 1921. Now in CP.
Notes on Euripides, Pausanias and Greek Lyric Poets. (1918-20) Beinecke Library, Yale University. (Abbreviated NEPG). One essay, 'The Wise Sappho' in NTV, 1982.
Paint it To-day. (1921) Beinecke Library, Yale University. (Abbreviated PIT.)
Heliodora and Other Poems. Boston, Houghton Mifflin, 1924. Now in CP.
Asphodel. (1921-22) Beinecke Library, Yale University.
Collected Poems of H.D. New York, Boni and Liveright, 1925. Now in CP.
Pilate's Wife. (1924 and through the 1920s) Beinecke Library, Yale University.
Hedylus. (1926) Redding Ridge, CT, Black Swan Books, 1980. Originally published 1928. (Abbreviated H.)
Palimpsest. (1925-26) Carbondale, Ill., Southern Illinois University Press, 1968. Originally published 1926. (Abbreviated P.)
Hippolytus Temporizes. Boston, Houghton Mifflin, 1927.
'The Cinema and the Classics [Three Essays]', *Close Up* I, 1 (July 1927): 22-33; 2 (August 1927): 30-9; 3 (November 1927): 18-31.
Her [HERmione]. (1927) New York, New Directions, 1981. (Abbreviated HER.)
'Narthex', *The [Second] American Caravan: A Yearbook of American Literature*, ed. Alfred Kreymborg, Lewis

Mumford, Paul Rosenfeld, New York, Macaulay, 1928: 225–84.

Red Roses for Bronze. London, Chatto and Windus, 1931.

The Usual Star (and *Two Americans*). Dijon, Imprimerie Darantière, 1934.

Kora and Ka (and *Mira-Mare*). Dijon, Imprimerie Darantière, 1934.

Nights. Dijon, Imprimerie Darantière, 1935.

The Hedgehog. (1924) London, Brendin Publishing Co., 1936.

Euripides' Ion. Boston, Houghton Mifflin, 1937.

The Dead Priestess Speaks. (1930s) Now in CP.

'A Note on Poetry', *The Oxford Anthology of American Literature,* ed. William Rose Benét and Norman Holmes Pearson, New York, Oxford University Press, 1938. Volume II: 1287–88.

Bid Me To Live (A Madrigal). (1939, 1949) Redding Ridge, CT., Black Swan Books, 1983. Originally published 1960. (Abbreviated BMTL.)

Within the Walls. (1940–41). Beinecke Library, Yale University.

The Gift. (1941–43) New York, New Directions, 1982 [abridged by Griselda Ohanessian]. Chapter 1, 'The Dark Room', including H.D.'s Notes, *Montemora* 8 (1981): 57–76. Chapter 3, 'The Dream', *Contemporary Literature* 10, 4 (Autumn 1969): 605–26. Chapter 2, 'Fortune Teller', *The Iowa Review*, 16, 2 (1986). (Abbreviated G.)

The Walls Do Not Fall [Part I, *Trilogy*]. (1942). Originally published 1944. New York, New Directions, 1973. Now in CP.

Majic Ring. (1943) Beinecke Library, Yale University.

Tribute to the Angels [Part II, *Trilogy*]. (1944). Originally published 1945. New York, New Directions, 1973. Now in CP.

Writing on the Wall [Major part of *Tribute to Freud*]. (1944) Originally published 1956. Boston, David R. Godine, 1974. (Abbreviated TF.)

The Flowering of the Rod [Part III, *Trilogy*]. (1944) Originally published 1946. New York, New Directions, 1973. Now in CP.

By Avon River. (1945–46) New York, Macmillan, 1949.

The Sword Went Out to Sea (*Synthesis of a Dream*). (1947) Beinecke Library, Yale University.

White Rose and the Red. (1948?) Beinecke Library, Yale University.

Advent [Revised journal (1933 and 1948) now part of *Tribute to Freud*]. Boston, David R. Godine, 1974. (Abbreviated TF.)

'Notes on Recent Writing'. (1949) Beinecke Library, Yale University. *The Iowa Review*, 16, 2 (1986). (Abbreviated NRW.)

Autobiographical Notes. (1949) Beinecke Library, Yale University.

The Mystery. (1951?) Beinecke Library, Yale University.

Helen in Egypt. (1952–56) New York, New Directions, 1974. Originally published 1961. (Abbreviated HE.)

Magic Mirror. (1955) Beinecke Library, Yale University.

Compassionate Friendship. (1955) Beinecke Library, Yale University. (Abbreviated CF.)

Hirslanden Notebooks. (1957–1959) Beinecke Library, Yale University.

The Selected Poems of H.D. New York, Grove Press, 1957.

Vale Ave. (1957) Beinecke Library, Yale University.

'Sagesse' [in *Hermetic Definition*]. (1957) New York, New Directions, 1972. (Abbreviated S.)

End to Torment. (1958) New York, New Directions, 1979. (Abbreviated ETT.)

'Winter Love' [in *Hermetic Definition*]. (1959) New York, Directions, 1972. (Abbreviated S.)

Thorn Thicket. (1960) Beinecke Library, Yale University. (Abbreviated TT.)

'Hermetic Definition' [in *Hermetic Definition*]. (1960–61) New York, New Directions, 1972. (Abbreviated HD.)

Collected Poems, 1912–1944. Edited by Louis L. Martz. New York, New Directions, 1983. (Abbreviated CP.)

H.D. Letters to Sylvia Dobson in 'A Friendship Traced: Letters to Sylvia Dobson', ed. Carol Tinker, *Conjunctions* 2 (1982): 115–57.

H.D. Letters to F.S.Flint in 'Selected Letters from H.D. to F.S.Flint: A Commentary on the Imagist Period', ed. Cyrena N.Pondrom, *Contemporary Literature* 10, 4 (Autumn 1969): 557–86.

H.D. Letter to Richard Johns in *A Return to Pagany: The History, Correspondence, and Selections from a Little Magazine, 1929–1932*, ed. Stephen Halpert with Richard Johns, Beacon Press, Boston, 1969, 444.

Secondary Sources

Abel, Elizabeth, ed. *Writing and Sexual Difference*, Chicago, The University of Chicago Press, 1982.

Aldington, Richard. *Collected Poems*, New York, Covici, Friede Publishers, 1928.

———. *Life for Life's Sake*, New York, Viking, 1941.

Arthur, Marylin. 'Psycho-Mythology: The Case of H.D.', *Bucknell Review* 28, 2 (1983): 65–79.

Auerbach, Nina. 'Magi and Maidens: The Romance of the Victorian Freud', in Abel, ed. *Writing and Sexual Difference*.

Beauvoir, Simone de. *The Second Sex* (1949), trans. H.M.Parshley, New York, Bantam Books, 1961.

Berger, John. *Ways of Seeing*, London, Penguin Books, 1972.

Bryher, Winifred. *Development, a novel*, London, Constable, 1920.

———. *Two Selves*, Paris, Contact Publishing, 1923.

———. *West*, London, Jonathan Cape, 1925.

———. *Civilians*, Territet, POOL, [1927].

———. *The Heart to Artemis; a Writer's Memoirs*, New York, Harcourt Brace and World, 1962.

———. *The Day of Mars, 1940–46*, New York, Harcourt Brace Jovanovich, 1972.

Buck, Claire. 'Freud and H.D.–bisexuality and a feminine discourse', *M/F* 8 (1983): 52–65.

———. *Freud and H.D.: Bi-sexuality and a Feminine Discourse*, Brighton, Harvester, forthcoming.

Burke, Carolyn. 'Introduction to Luce Irigaray's "When Our Lips Speak Together" *Signs* 6,1 (Autumn 1980): 66–8.

———. 'Supposed Persons: Modernist Poetry and the Female Subject [a Review Essay]', *Feminist Studies* 11, 1 (Spring 1985): 131–46.

Chevigny, Bell Gale. 'Daughters Writing: Toward a Theory of Women's Biography', in *Between Women*, ed. Carol Ascher, Louise DeSalvo, Sara Ruddick, Boston, Beacon Press, 1984: 357–79.

Cixous, Hélène. 'The Laugh of the Medusa', trans. Keith and Paula Cohen in *New French Feminisms*, ed. Elaine Marks and Isabelle de Courtivron, Amherst, The University of Massachusetts Press, 1980: 245–64.

Collecott, Diana. 'Remembering oneself: the reputation and later poetry of H.D.' *Critical Quarterly* 27 (1985): 7–22.

———. 'Images at the Crossroads: The "H.D. Scrapbook" ', in King, ed. *H.D.: Woman and Poet*.

Cook, Blanche Wiesen. '"Women Alone Stir My Imagination": Lesbianism and the Cultural Tradition', *Signs* 4, 4 (Summer 1979): 647–62.

De Lauretis, Teresa. *Alice Doesn't: Feminism, Semiotics, Cinema*, Bloomington, Indiana University Press, 1984.

Dembo, L.S. *Conceptions of Reality in Modern American Poetry*, Berkeley, University of California Press, 1966.

Dinnerstein, Dorothy. *The Mermaid and the Minotaur: Sexual Arrangements and Human Malaise*, New York, Harper & Row, Publishers, 1976.

Duncan, Robert. *The H.D. Book* [the following based on Robert Duncan's own outline and chronology of publication to date, in *Ironwood* 22].

———. Part I, Chapter 1, *Coyote's Journal* 5–6 (1966): 8–31.

———. Part I, Chapter 2, *Coyote's Journal* 8 (1967): 27–35.

――――. Part I, Chapter 3, *Tri-Quarterly* 12 (Spring 1968): 67–82.

――――. Part I, Chapter 4, *Tri-Quarterly* 12 (Spring 1968): 82–98.

――――. Part I, Chapter 5, 'Occult Matters', *Stony Brook* 1 (Fall 1968): 4–19.

――――. Part I, Chapter 6 'Rites of Participation', *Caterpillar* 1 (October 1967): 6–29 and *Caterpillar* 2 (January 1968): 125–54.

――――. Part II, Chapter 1, *Sumac* I, 1 (Fall 1968): 101–46.

――――. Part II, Chapter 2, *Caterpillar* 6 (January 1969): 16–38.

――――. Part II, Chapter 3, *IO* 6 (Summer 1969): 1–10.

――――. Part II, Chapter 4, *Caterpillar* 7 (April 1969): 27–60.

――――. Part II, Chapter 5, sections in *Stony Brook* 3/4 (Fall 1969): 336–47, in *Credences* 2 (August 1975): 50–2, and in *Sagetrieb* 4, 2/3 (Fall & Winter 1985): 39–85.

――――. Part II, Chapter 6, *The Southern Review* 21, 1 (Jan. 1985): 26–48.

――――. Part II, Chapter 7, *Credences* 2 (1975): 53–67.

――――. Part II, Chapter 8, *Credences* 2 (1975): 68–94.

――――. Part II, Chapter 9, *Chicago Review* 30, 3 (Winter 1979): 37–88.

――――. Part II, Chapter 10, *Ironwood* 22 (1983): 47–64.

――――. Part II, Chapter 11, *Montemora* 8 (1981): 79–113.

DuPlessis, Rachel Blau. 'Romantic Thralldom in H.D.', *Contemporary Literature* 20, 2 (Summer 1979): 178–203.

――――. 'Family, Sexes, Psyche: an essay on H.D. and the muse of the woman writer', *Montemora* 6 (1979): 137–56.

――――. 'A Note on the State of H.D.'s *The Gift*', *Sulfur* 9 (1984): 178–82.

――――. 'For the Etruscans' (1979), in *The New Feminist Criticism*, ed. Elaine Showalter.

――――. *Writing Beyond the Ending: Narrative Strategies of Twentieth-Century Women Writers*, Bloomington, Indiana University Press, 1985.

———— and Susan Stanford Friedman, '"Woman is Perfect": H.D.'s Debate with Freud', *Feminist Studies* 7, 3 (Fall 1981): 417–30.

Field, Kenneth. 'Introduction,' in H.D., *Tribute to Freud*. Boston, David R. Godine, 1974: xvii–xlv.

Firchow, Peter E. 'Rico and Julia: The Hilda Doolittle–D. H. Lawrence Affair Reconsidered', *Journal of Modern Literature* 8, 1 (1980): 51–76.

Freibert, Lucy. 'Conflict and Creativity in the World of H.D.', *Journal of Women's Studies in Literature*, 1, 3 (Summer 1979): 258–71.

————. 'From Semblance to Selfhood: The Evolution of Woman in H.D.'s Neo-Epic *Helen in Egypt*', *Arizona Quarterly* 36 (1980): 165–75.

Friedberg, Anne. 'Approaching *Borderline*', *Millenium Film Journal* 7–9 (Fall–Winter 1980–81): 130–9.

Friedman, Susan Stanford. 'Who Buried H.D.? A Poet, Her Critics, and Her Place in "The Literary Tradition"', *College English* 36, 7 (March 1975): 801–14.

————. 'Creating a Woman's Mythology: H.D.'s *Helen in Egypt*', *Women's Studies* 5, 2 (1977): 163–98.

————. 'Psyche Reborn: Tradition. Re-Vision, and the Goddess as Mother-Symbol in H.D.'s Epic Poetry', *Women's Studies* 6, 2 (1979): 147–60.

————. *Psyche Reborn: The Emergence of H.D.*, Bloomington, Indiana University Press, 1981.

————. '"I go where I love": An Intertextual Study of H.D. and Adrienne Rich', *Signs* 9, 2 (Winter 1983): 228–245.

————. '"Remembering Shakespeare Always, But Remembering him Differently": H.D.'s *By Avon River*', *Sagetrieb* 2, 2 (Summer–Fall 1983), 45–70.

————. 'H.D. [Review of Barbara Guest, *Herself Defined*]', *Contemporary Literature* 26, 1 (Spring 1985): 107–13.

————. 'Palimpsests of Origin in H.D.'s Career', forthcoming, *Poesis* 6 (Fall 1985).

————. 'Ghost Stories: H.D.'s *Hedylus*'. *Sagetrieb* 4, 2/3 (Fall & Winter 1985): 325–33.

H.D.

——. 'H.D.', *Dictionary of Literary Biography: Modern American Poets*. Detroit: Gale Research, forthcoming, 1986.

——. 'The Modernism of "The Scattered Remnant": Race and Politics in H.D.'s Development', forthcoming in King, ed., *H.D.: Woman and Poet*, Orono, National Poetry Foundation, 1986.

——. *Sagas of the Self: A Study of H.D.'s Prose*, forthcoming, Cambridge University Press.

——, ed. with an introduction. *Portrait of an Analysis with Freud: H.D.-Bryher Letters, 1933–34*, forthcoming.

—— and Rachel Blau DuPlessis. '"I Had Two Loves Separate": The Sexualities of H.D.'s *Her*', *Montemora* 8 (1981): 7–30.

Gelpi, Albert. 'Hilda in Egypt', *The Southern Review* 18, 2 (Spring 1982): 233–50.

——. 'The Thistle and the Serpent', in H.D., *Notes on Thought and Vision*, San Francisco, City Lights Books, 1982: 7–14.

Gilbert, Sandra. 'H.D.? Who Was She?', *Contemporary Literature* 24, 4 (Winter 1983): 496–511.

—— and Susan Gubar. *The Madwoman in the Attic:The Woman Writer and the Nineteenth-Century Literary Imagination*, New Haven, Yale University Press, 1979.

—— and Susan Gubar. *Shakespeare's Sisters: Feminist Essays on Women Poets*, Bloomington, Indiana University Press, 1979.

Guber, Susan. 'The Echoing Spell of H.D.'s Trilogy', in *Shakespeare's Sisters*, ed. Gilbert and Gubar: 200–18.

——. 'The Birth of the Artist as Heroine: (Re) production, the *Kunstlerroman* Tradition, and the Fiction of Katherine Mansfield', in *The Representation of Women in Fiction*, ed. Carolyn G.Heilbrun and Margaret R.Higonnet, Baltimore, The Johns Hopkins University Press, 1983.

——. '"The Blank Page" and the Issues of Female Creativity' in *The New Feminist Criticism*, ed. Elaine Showalter: 292–313.

——. 'Sapphistries', *Signs* 10, 1 (Autumn 1984): 43–62.

Guest, Barbara. *Herself Defined: The Poet H.D. and Her World*, New York, Doubleday, 1984.

Holland, Norman. 'H.D. and the "Blameless Physician"', *Contemporary Literature* 10, 4 (Autumn 1969): 474–506.

——. *Poems in Persons: An Introduction to the Psychoanalysis of Literature*, New York, W.W.Norton, 1973.

Homans, Margaret. *Women Writers and Poetic Identity: Dorothy Wordsworth, Emily Brontë and Emily Dickinson*, Princeton, Princeton University Press, 1980.

Hughes, Glenn. *Imagism and the Imagists. A Study in Modern Poetry*, Stanford, Stanford University Press, 1931.

Irigaray, Luce. *This Sex Which is Not One* (1977), trans. Catherine Porter with Carolyn Burke, Ithaca, Cornell University Press, 1985.

Jacobus, Mary. 'The Question of Language: Men of Maxims and *The Mill on the Floss*', in *Writing and Sexual Difference*, ed. Elizabeth Abel.

——, ed. *Women Writing and Writing about Women*, London, Croom Helm, 1979.

Jardine, Alice. 'Pre-Texts for the Transatlantic Feminist', *Yale French Studies* 62 (1981): 220–36.

——. 'Gynesis', *Diacritics* 12 (Summer 1982): 54–65.

Jehlen, Myra. 'Archimedes and the Paradox of Feminist Criticism', *Signs* 6, 4 (Summer 1981): 575–601.

Juhasz, Suzanne. *Naked and Fiery Forms: Modern American Poetry by Women: A New Tradition*, New York, Harper & Row, 1976.

Kammer, Jeanne. 'The Art of Silence and the Forms of Women's Poetry', in *Shakespeare's Sisters*, ed. Gilbert and Gubar: 153–64.

Kaplan, Cora. 'Language and Gender', *Papers on Patriarchy* (Conference, London 1976), Brighton, Women's Publishing Collective, 1976: 21–37.

Kerblat, Jeanne. '"The Rose Loved of Lover" or the Heroines in the Poems of the Twenties by H.D.', *GRENA* (Aix-en-Provence, 1981): 45–64.

King, Michael. 'Foreword', in H.D., *End to Torment*, New

York, New Directions, 1979: vii–xii.

———, ed. *H.D.: Woman and Poet*, Orono, National Poetry Foundation, 1986.

Kloepfer, Deborah Kelly. 'Flesh Made Word: Maternal Inscription in H.D.', *Sagetrieb* 3, 1 (Spring 1984): 27–48.

Kolodny, Annette. 'Dancing Through the Minefield: Some Observations on the Theory, Practice and Politics of a Feminist Literary Criticism' in *The New Feminist Criticism*, Showalter, ed.: 144–67.

———. 'A Map for Rereading: Gender and the Interpretation of Literary Texts', in Showalter, ed.: 46–62.

Kristeva, Julia. *Desire in Language: A Semiotic Approach to Literature and Art*, trans. T.Gora, A.Jardine, L.Roudiez, New York, Columbia University Press, 1980.

Levertov, Denise. 'H.D.: An Appreciation' (1962), in *The Poet in the World*, New York, New Directions, 1973: 244–8.

Mandel, Charlotte. 'Garbo/Helen: The Self-Projection of Beauty by H.D.', *Women's Studies* 7, 2–3 (1980): 127–35.

———. 'Magical Lenses: Poet's Vision Beyond the Naked Eye', in *H.D.: Woman and Poet*, ed. Michael King, Orono, National Poetry Foundation, forthcoming.

Martz, Louis. 'Introduction', in H.D., *Collected Poems, 1912–1944*, New York, New Directions, 1983: xi–xxxvi.

Miller, Nancy. 'Emphasis Added: Plots and Plausibilities in Women's Fiction', in *The New Feminist Criticism*, Showalter, ed.: 339–60.

Morris, Adalaide. 'Reading H.D.'s "Helios and Athene"', *Iowa Review* 12, 2–3 (Spring–Summer 1981): 155–64.

———. 'The Concept of Projection: H.D.'s Visionary Powers', *Contemporary Literature* 25, 4 (Winter 1984): 411–36.

———. *H.D.'s Lexicon*, Indiana University Press, forthcoming.

Ostriker, Alicia. 'The Thieves of Language: Women Poets and Revisionist Mythmaking', *Signs* 8, 1

(Autumn 1982): 68–90.

———. *Writing Like a Woman*, Ann Arbor, University of Michigan Press, 1983.

———. *Stealing the Language: The Emergence of Women's Poetry in America*, Boston, Beacon Press, 1986.

Pearson, Norman Holmes, 'An Interview on H.D.' with L.S.Dembo, *Contemporary Literature* 10, 4 (Autumn 1969): 435–46.

———. 'Foreword', in H.D., *Trilogy*, New York, New Directions, 1973: v–xii.

———. "Foreword', in H.D., *Hermetic Definition*, New York, New Directions, 1972: [v–viii].

Peck, John. 'Passio Perpetuae H.D.', *Parnassus* 3 (Spring–Summer 1975): 42–75.

Pondrom, Cyrena N. 'H.D. and the Origins of Imagism', *Sagetrieb* 4, 1 (1985): 73–97.

Pound, Ezra. *The Cantos of Ezra Pound*, New York, New Directions, 1948.

———. *The Letters of Ezra Pound, 1907–1941*, edited D.D.Paige, New York, Harcourt, Brace and World, 1950.

Quinn, Vincent. *Hilda Doolittle (H.D.)*, New York, Twayne Publishers, Inc., 1967.

———. 'H.D.'s "Hermetic Definition": The Poet as Archetypal Mother', *Contemporary Literature* 18, 1 (Winter 1977): 51–61.

Rasula, Jed. 'A Renaissance of Women Writers', *Sulfur* 7 (1983) 160–72.

Rich, Adrienne. *On Lies, Secrets, and Silence: Selected Prose 1966–1978*, New York, W.W. Norton, 1979.

———. 'Compulsory Heterosexuality and Lesbian Existence', *Signs* 5, 4 (Summer 1980): 631–60.

Riddel, Joseph. 'H.D. and the Poetics of "Spiritual Realism" ', *Contemporary Literature* 10, 4 (Autumn 1969): 447–73.

———. 'H.D.'s Scene of Writing – Poetry as (AND) Analysis', *Studies in the Literary Imagination* 12, 1 (Spring 1979): 41–59.

H.D.

Robinson, Janice S. *H.D.: The Life and Work of an American Poet*, Boston, Houghton Mifflin, 1982.

Schaffner, Perdita, 'Merano, 1962', *Paideuma* 4, 2–3 (Fall–Winter 1975): 513–18.

———. 'The Egyptian Cat', in H.D. *Hedylus*, (Redding Ridge, CT, Black Swan Books, 1980): 142–46.

———. 'Pandora's Box', in H.D., *HERmione*, New York, New Directions, 1981: vii–xi.

———. 'Unless a Bomb Falls . . .' in H.D. *The Gift*, New York, New Directions, 1982: ix–xv.

———. 'A Profound Animal', in H.D., *Bid Me to Live*, Redding Ridge, CT, Black Swan Books, 1983: 185–94.

Showalter, Elaine (ed.), *The New Feminist Criticism: Essays on Women, Literature, and Theory*, New York, Pantheon Books, 1985.

———. 'Feminist Criticism in the Wilderness', in Elaine Showalter (ed.), *New Feminist Criticism*: 243–70.

Smith, Paul, *Pound Revised*, London, Croom Helm, 1983.

Swann, Thomas Burnett. *The Classical World of H.D.*, Lincoln, University of Nebraska Press, 1962.

Tinker, Carol, ed. 'A Friendship Traced; [H.D.] Letters to Sylvia Dobson', *Conjunctions* 2 (1982): 115–57.

Wagner, Linda Welshimer. '*Helen in Egypt*: A Culmination', *Contemporary Literature* 10, 4 (Autumn 1969): 523–36.

Walsh, John. 'Afterword' and 'Notes on the Text' in H.D., *Hedylus*, Redding Ridge, CT, Black Swan Books, 1982: 147–56.

———. 'Afterword' and 'A Note on the Text', in H.D., *Hippolytus Temporizes*, Redding Ridge, CT, Black Swan Books, 1985.

———. 'Afterword' and 'A Note on the Text', in H.D., *Ion*, Redding Ridge, CT., Black Swan Books, 1985.

———. 'Afterword', in H.D., *By Avon River*, Redding Ridge, CT., Black Swan Books, 1986.

Woolf, Virginia. *A Room of One's Own* (1929), New York, Harcourt Brace and World, 1957.

———. 'Women and Fiction', *Granite and Rainbow*, New

York, Harcourt Brace and Company, 1958.
———. 'Professions for Women', *Collected Essays, Volume II*, New York, Harcourt Brace and World, 1967.

Both *Contemporary Literature* (guest editors, Susan Stanford Friedman and Rachel Blau DuPlessis) and *The Iowa Review* (guest editor, Adalaide Morris) have special issues for the H.D. centennial year, 1986.

Index

164

Index